CHOICES
ARE
FORERUNNERS

CHOICES ARE FORERUNNERS

A Complete Guide
to Making Better Choices

EVELYN EKHATOR

XULON PRESS

Xulon Press
2301 Lucien Way #415
Maitland, FL 32751
407.339.4217
www.xulonpress.com

© 2021 by Evelyn Ekhator

All rights reserved solely by the author. The author guarantees all contents are original and do not infringe upon the legal rights of any other person or work. No part of this book may be reproduced in any form without the permission of the author. The views expressed in this book are not necessarily those of the publisher.

Due to the changing nature of the Internet, if there are any web addresses, links, or URLs included in this manuscript, these may have been altered and may no longer be accessible. The views and opinions shared in this book belong solely to the author and do not necessarily reflect those of the publisher. The publisher therefore disclaims responsibility for the views or opinions expressed within the work.

Paperback ISBN-13: 978-1-6628-1561-4
Hard Cover ISBN-13: 978-1-6628-1562-1
Ebook ISBN-13: 978-1-6628-1563-8

DEDICATION

THIS BOOK IS dedicated to my beloved mother. Mrs. Esther A Omoruyi, who passed on to glory during the publishing of this book. She was my first teacher who taught me the ways of life and led me to Jesus Christ.

My mother's footprints in my life are indelible. Her voice of wisdom, discipline, and love is still speaking even when she is gone. It is a great honor for me to call you my mother. Thank you iye (AKA iye Evelyn) for your love, support, and prayers.

You were always a blessing and solution to those who came in contact with you. I miss you, my dear mother.

TABLE OF CONTENTS

Introduction xi

Chapter 1: Choices. 1
    Choice-Making Is Crucial 1
    Is Real Neutrality in The Maze of Choices? 3
    Power of Our Choices 3
    Diversity in the Maze of Choices 4
    Choices Are Universal 5
    What Is a Choice? 5
    Choices Are Raw Materials. 6
    Choices Produce Positive and Negative Outcomes 7
    Significant Choices vs. Trivial Choices vs. Grievous Choices 7
    Life Always Present Options 9
    The Difference between Choices and Decisions 10

Chapter 2: Choices Determine Capacity 13
    Choices Influence Capacity 15
    Capacity Influences Choice 16
    Barrage of Choices 18
    Our Choices Influence Our Future 19
    The Propulsion of Internal and External Conditions 20
    We Are Responsible for Our Choices. 20

CHOICES ARE FORERUNNERS

- Our Choices Are Reflective 21
- Active and Passive Actions 22
- Active, Inactive, and Dormant Choices 22
- Choice Equations 24

Chapter 3: Choices Have Rewards or Consequences 27
- Choices Are Like Seeds 28
- The Due Season of Choices 29
- The Harvest of Choices 30
- Good, Right, Bad, Poor, and Wrong Choices 32
- Bad Choices 32
- Wrong Choices 33
- Right Choices 33
- Good Choices 34
- Choices Are Emissaries 35
- Our Choices Reveal Content 35
- Choices Are Transmitted through Different Channels 36
- Engaging the Future through Choices 37
- Rewards and Punishments Are the Outcome of Choices .. 38

Chapter 4: The Choice Meter 41
- Choice Meter Readings 42
- Choice Cycle 43
- The Life Highway 43
- Choices Controls Traffic 44
- Choices Can Elevate, Direct, or Derail 45
- The Current of Choice 45

Chapter 5: Common Grounds 49
- Different Types of Common Ground 50
- Time Is Invaluable 56

Chapter 6: Choices Are Invitations 61
- Choices Are Accessories 63
- Choices: The Place of Freedom 64
- The Maze of Choice Is a Maze of Selection 65
- The Freedom to Choose Empowers Us 66

TABLE OF CONTENTS

    Choices Are Investments 66

Chapter 7: By Choice 69
    Premediated and Impromptu Choices 89

Chapter 8: The Maze of Choices 93

Chapter 9: The Journey of Choices 103
    The Pathway of Choices 104
    Choices Are Forerunners 105
    Life Is Lived Based on a Combination of Choices 108
    Choices Are Connectors 109
    Our Choices Are a Launching Pad 110
    Choices Position and Reposition 111
    Choices Nurture or Devour 112
    Choices Are an Individual and Collective Responsibility 113
    The Choices We Make Foster Something in Our Lives 114

Chapter 10: Determinant of Choices 117
    Primary Determinant of Choice 129
    Our Choices Are Our Responsibilities 130

Chapter 11: Operative Dimensions of Choice 133
    Operative Dimensions of Choices 134

Chapter 12: Choices Govern All 169

Chapter 13: Be Mindful 179

Chapter 14: Choose YE 193
    The Choices We Make Are Deposits 196
    Our Choices Are Our Life Navigators 198
    The Choice Reunion 202
    Choices Are Agents of Change 204
    Choices Are Time Oriented 206

Daily Choice Nuggets 215

INTRODUCTION

IN LIFE'S JOURNEY, the choices we all make in different areas of our lives never disappear but go ahead of us into our tomorrow, our future. They trigger the events and happenings that transpire in our lives, which eventually produce our outcomes, results, and experiences in life. Every choice we make acts as our messenger for the future to prepare the way for us as our forerunner.

Therefore, choices are our forerunners of the events that transpire in our future, and at every junction in life's journey, the choices of yesterday always show up to interfere with today's activities and results to either promote, advertise, encourage, empower or stagnate, derail, or become a thorn in our flesh. That is how powerful choices are in commanding and determining what transpires in our lives and what we become in life. One way or another, there is always a reunion between us and the choices we made in the past.

Most times, we are not usually prepared or ready for the reunion with the choices we've made in the past, especially the poor, bad, and ill choices; but when the choices we've made in the past are good or profitable there is always excitement and high expectations in reuniting with the choices from our past.

CHOICES ARE FORERUNNERS

Whether we are engaging in making good or bad choices, the truth is once the choices we've made in the past show up in our future, those choices have the power to determine our welfare, progress, position, and location. Wherever we might be today, personally or collectively as a group—whether in the pinnacle of our field or at the bottom—is a reflection of the choices we've made in the past and sometimes the choices other people made on our behalves. Therefore, the choices we made in the past have the power to position us today as a frontliner, a trailblazer, a legend, a participant, or as a spectator on the sidelines of life.

If we are not satisfied with our present positions, locations, or situations in life, it is our choices today that will determine whether we will be stuck with our present situations and experiences or we will transition out of the current situation. In the Maze of Choices, it is very vital to be conscious of the fact that the choices we make daily are our forerunners that go into our futures, awaiting our arrivals to finally determine our lots or fates in life. Hence, it is crucial to us as humans to choose aright, because the choices we make in different spheres of life are our navigators in the race of life. Choices have the power to control our lives—change our positions, locations, situations, results, and experiences.

CHAPTER 1

CHOICES

LIFE IS A compilation of choices, and we live our lives on the bases of the choices we've made or refused to make. While Choices are made consciously and subconsciously in the Maze of Choices, the choices we make consciously or subconsciously always set a wheel in motion in our lives to create the events and happenings that transpire in our lives.

In the Maze of Choices, there is no neutral area because choosing not to make a choice is a choice made already. None of us can live our lives without making choices. Choice-making is as crucial to our human existence as the food we eat and the air we breathe. Choice-making in all spheres of life is the oxygen and nutrients that trigger, sustain, and maintain all activities in the streets of life.

The choices we make can either enhance or diminish the quality and longevity of our lives.

Choice-Making Is Crucial

Choice-making is a crucial part of our existence as humans. We are called upon every day to make choices in all affairs of life and to live by the choices we make. Every day, life throws us options to choose from and opportunities to make choices about. These options can be openings, determinants, or catalysts for greatness or failure. The outcome of each choice depends on the choice we choose to make amid the multiple options available.

In the Maze of Choices, we are confronted with multiple choices embedded with opportunities, possibilities, advantages, or disadvantages, which can yield positive or negative outcomes known as rewards or consequences.

All humans make choices; it is not exclusive to any race or group. Both the young, old, learned, or unlearned, make choices. Just as oxygen is crucial to our existence, likewise, is choice-making; it is impossible to live our lives without making choices. It is impossible as human beings to ignore the power of choices and the freedom to choose.

The power to choose is as powerful as the oxygen we breathe. Just as there is no human being who can exist without breathing in oxygen, there is no human being who will go through life without making choices in all areas of life. That is why choice-making is crucial and important for our survival as human beings.

There is no aspect of life where choices are left out. In all issues of life, it is impossible not to make choices. Even when we choose not to make a choice in any given issue, we have indirectly and subconsciously made a choice. At any point in life, it is a choice when we choose to do nothing; that is how crucial choices are. Doing nothing about a particular issue in our lives that needs to be addressed is a choice. There is no neutral ground in the Maze of Choices. In any sphere of life, there is really no such thing as choosing to stay neutral, because the place of neutrality is a place where we are relinquishing our power of choice to others subconsciously and empowering them to choose for us.

Is Real Neutrality in The Maze of Choices?

In the Maze of Choices, choices are never neutral, even when we choose to stay neutral by not choosing in any given situation. Whether we are aware of it or not, we are indirectly making choices that might have good or bad impacts in our lives. In any situation when we choose not to utilize our power of choice, we have consciously and subconsciously made a choice to either empower the positive or negative side of the situation. Staying neutral by not making a choice is actually a choice—because being neutral in any situation is relinquishing our power of choice to the side of the situation, which might eventually triumph over the other, either to our advantage or disadvantage depending on the outcome of the choices that were made. Since remaining neutral by not making choices in any situation is a choice in itself, it is crucial for us to be aware of how the choices we make daily affect and impact our lives and others around us. In the race of life and the Maze of Choices, there is no neutral ground, neither are there spectators in the Maze of Choices. We all are participants who are actively engaging our power of choice consciously and subconsciously.

We should never underestimate the power and impact of the choices we make. The choices we make matter even in trivial things of life, as the choices we make have the power to create series of events in our lives that might be profitable or detrimental to us.

Power of Our Choices

There is power in the choices we make to create the events and happenings in our lives and sometimes in the lives of others. The choices we've made reflect in all areas of our lives as our realities. Our power of choice is our freedom to choose whatever route we want to embark on in any issue and situation of life, which will eventually become our lot in life. Choice is an aspect of life many of us take for granted. Often, we do not realize that the choices we make today are forerunners of all transactions and events of tomorrow. The choices we make in life have the power to promote, create opportunities and possibilities, destroy, derail, sustain, stagnate, kill, or keep us alive. Likewise, it is important to know that the choices other people make have the power to change the course of their lives, for better or worse. In all realms of life, the choices we make always sets in motion a chain reaction of rewards or consequences which can affect everyone within our sphere of influence.

It is critical to know and understand how the power of choice dominates in all aspects of human existence. The choices we make set in motion the course and direction of our lives and that of others. One wrong choice can affect generations to come, not just an individual but a family, a community, a nation, and generations to come. With this in mind, it is disheartening to see some people choose to ignore the power of choice in their lives.

Diversity in the Maze of Choices

In the Maze of Choices, there are different groups of people and the power to choose that is within each of us is being utilized differently by these people and groups. The use of our power to choose in life differs from person to person and from situation to situation. Some people are not aware of how their choices affect and control the course of their lives, while others have gained some insight on how their choices impact their lives. People utilize their power of choice to their own advantage, based on their knowledge and understanding. Consciously and subconsciously, some of us are utilizing our power of choice to set our route and cruise through our lives judiciously, while some of us are not fully maximizing our power of choice in our daily endeavors. However, our awareness of the inherent power embedded in the choices we make in different areas of life, and the effect our choices can have on us and others, will certainly influence the choices we make in any situation of life.

> **The choices we make become the events and happenings that transpire in the streets of life.**

Choices Are Universal

Choice-making is universal and common to all human beings, and the choices we made in all issues of life are translated into the events and transactions that transpire in the streets of life. Our choices are the tools we use to create our future. Also, they can become a weapon we use against ourselves and others who come in contact with us.

In the streets of life, choices are everything. Choices are the common denominator in all realms of life. We use them to negotiate and possess things. Choices are our universal GPS, which we all use daily to route and reroute our steps in all spheres of life. As we walk the streets of life in our different endeavors, the choices we make daily become our selection power to directly or indirectly control what transpires in our lives. Therefore, all transactions in the streets of life are sponsored by the choices we make daily. Our choices form the baseline for our lives. Every choice we make in life is laying a foundation that other choices are built on, and each choice has the inherent power to initiate more choices in every situation in life.

In every aspect of life, we are always presented with alternatives to choose from, and sometimes these alternatives might not necessarily be what we want, but they can be lifesaving alternatives.

What Is a Choice?

A choice simply means the act of choosing something. We make choices when we are presented with a range of options to choose from. Even in bad or painful situations, the power to choose is always present. Choices select options in every situation, even in the most impossible situations of life.

Choices are the hinges that swing all doors open or closed in life, and the choices we make control all doors in our lives. In any sphere of life, the choices we make can open or close doors of opportunities, possibilities, unity, peace, friendship, and more.

CHOICES ARE FORERUNNERS

Choices are the central point on which every aspect of our lives depends, because the power to choose the path we want to embark on in all spheres of life is always active in our lives, especially when dealing with ourselves and others. It is vital to have it engraved in our hearts, and always remember that the choices we make have the power to create a chain reaction. Every choice made always creates an atmosphere for us to make more choices. Which creates a chain reaction, which evolves around, and in our lives and in the lives of others. That is why it is crucial not to make choices carelessly, because the choices we've made are the raw materials we use to build and live our lives.

The choices we make are raw materials that are processed into outcomes, events, and experiences in our lives.

Choices Are Raw Materials

Choices are the vital raw materials that are necessary in creating the events and happenings in our lives as humans. The choices we make daily produce a finish product(s). The finish product(s) can be seen under the label of rewards or consequences. Sometimes, the choices we make can produce a single product or multiple products. It all depends on the gravity of the choice and what the choice made entails.

Just as manufacturing companies uses raw materials to produces their goods or products, we as human beings are actively using the choices, we make daily as raw materials to produce different products in our lives and sometimes in the lives of others. The alarming side of choices being raw materials for future events is that people can be impacted by the outcome of the choices made by another person without them having any power to exempt themselves from the impact of the choice made by that other person.

For example, when we choose hatred as a raw material, it will always produce violence and discord. When anger is chosen as a raw material, the end product is lack of self-control, but when love is chosen as our raw material in our dealings, it produces different outcomes, like peace, unity, harmony, acceptance, and kindness. The end products of choices as raw materials are rewards or consequences that are embedded in the events and happenings we experience as humans.

Choices Produce Positive and Negative Outcomes

The choices we make can produce either rewards or consequences, which can also be called positive or negative outcomes. The positive or negative outcomes are the attributes of the choices we make. These attributes radiate and reflect back on us and other people within the circle of our influence.

When the choices we make carry elements of positive attributes, those choices result in peace, joy, and healthy vibes, but when the attributes of our choices are negative, the choices generate negative vibes of discomfort, toxic flow, contention, and anarchy. It is vital to see each choice as a means to a power end that will make a difference and have a tremendous effect in our lives and on the lives of others.

With this consciously and vividly engraved in our hearts, it will propel every one of us to make the right choice. This is because the choices we make or refuse to make daily affect all aspects of our lives. Since the choices we make today connect us to our tomorrow, it is very important to understand just how powerful our choices can be in orchestrating our outcomes in life.

Significant Choices vs. Trivial Choices vs. Grievous Choices

Some choices can be significant, trivial, or grievous in nature depending on what the choice made entails and the intent of the heart of the one making the choice. There are many visible and invisible factors that determine the outcomes of our choices.

CHOICES ARE FORERUNNERS

These visible and invisible factors are the reasons why our choices produce different outcomes. Even if a group of people makes the same kind of choices in the same settings, the choices made can have significant, trivial, or grievous outcomes because of these visible and invisible factors.

Some of the factors that influence the nature of our choices are

- Affluences
- Association
- Character
- Followers
- Influence
- Mindset (Mentality)
- Occupation and/or Profession
- Office
- Position
- Social Status
- Spirituality and Spiritual Strength

These factors above make our choices significant, trivial, or grievous. That is why our positions, statuses, and the offices we occupy in the society or within a family have a way of magnifying the choices we make. In certain areas of life, the effect and impact of our choices are directly proportional to the positions we occupy in a family or societal hierarchy, and our position or status in a family or society will determine the impact the choices we make create.

It is crucial to be sensitive of the effects and results of our choices, especially how they affect families or society. For example, the choices made by a father, mother, teacher, executive, prime minister, president, pastor, and musician can have significant impacts on those in their spheres of influence. In fact, their choices can create chain reactions and domino effects that impact all of society. It is important for parents, those in authority, and public figures to be aware of the choices they make regarding their choice words, what they eat, wear, and how they act, because their actions can inadvertently impact many people who look up to them.

For example, what a regular person chooses to eat, wear, or do might not influence or affect others when the person involved has no direct influence or link over those they come in contact with. However, in a situation where the individual is in a position of leadership, then the choices the person makes become significant because they have the power to influence others, which can result in profitable, significant, or grievous outcomes. To avoid making bad choices as a leader, it is crucial not to make choices carelessly or flippantly.

Life Always Present Options

In every situation, we all are always presented with options. There are always multiple options to choose from, and whatever we choose becomes our choice.

Even in the midst of difficult situations, happenings, and events, life presents to us the privilege and opportunity to choose. Whatever we choose becomes our choice, and we are solemnly responsible for the choices we make in spite of the circumstances that might influence our choices.

Choice Options Table

Love	Tenderness	Warmth	Devotion	Hate	Despise	Abhor
Nurture	Nourish	Support	Cultivate	Neglect	Ignore	Deprive
Respect	Esteem	Adore	Honor	Disrespect	Disdain	Dishonor
Serve	Assist	Succor	Help	Hinder	Impede	Frustrate
Impact	Transform	Shape	Modify	Crush	Derail	Abuse
Influence	Inspire	Impress	Mold	Incapacity	Impede	Thwart

CHOICES ARE FORERUNNERS

Accept	Acknowledge	Receive	Recognize	Reject	Abjure	Deny
Lawful	Legal	Licit	Authorized	Illicit	Unlawful	Prohibit
Empower	Emancipate	Build up	Liberate	Restrain	Belittle	Enslave
Encourage	Animate	Boost	Enhearten	Discourage	Dispirit	Demoralize
Meek	Humble	Peaceful	Modest	Proud	Arrogant	Snobbish
Kind	Amiable	Generous	Sympathetic	egocentric	Selfish	Cruel
Bold	Brave	Strong	Tough	Timid	Weak	Troubled
Calm	Peaceful	Quite	Poise	Forceful	Hostile	Aggressive
Act	Undertake	Conduct	Delay	Postpone	Halt	Procrastinate

At one point or another in the race of life, people, places, and situations can all influence us to choose any of the above choices. Whatever we choose becomes our choice regarding every particular issue or situation. This is irrespective of the propelling factors that might influence our decisions

Decisions are born when we make choices.

The Difference between Choices and Decisions

As stated before, the act of choosing from a range of available options is a choice, while a decision is the conclusion or resolution reached regarding a future action. Choices birth decisions, which set in motion a process based on the choice made. Choices are the common denominator of the decision- making process. On the other hand, decisions are enforced by actions which eventually cause reactions, and these reactions always produce results and results transmit feedback in the form of rewards or consequences.

Our choices showcase our preference in any situation.

> The choices we make have the power to make us the victim of circumstance or the crème de la crème of the society.

CHAPTER 2

CHOICES DETERMINE CAPACITY

Capacity is not static; it has the power to grow and increase, depending on the choices we make.

THE CHOICES WE make today determine the capacity we create and the space we access tomorrow. Our choices today are the forerunners of future actions and reactions. The choices we make to some extent determine and impact our financial, physical, social, and spiritual capacities in all realms of life. They eventually control the inflows and the spillages we experience in all spheres of life. Our choices either increase or decrease our capacity. This affects what eventually transpires in our lives and the results we experience in life.

In times of challenge, our ability to tackle the challenges of life is directly proportional to our capacity to handle them. The strength of our capacity to handle any issue is anchored on the choices we've made in the past and the choices we are making now.

According to some people, challenges have no timetable. As such, we must live prepared at all times for whatever life may throw at us. We can only be prepared for what happens tomorrow by the choices we make today. The choices we make today will determine if we have the capacity to handle the challenges we currently face along with the unknown challenges of tomorrow.

In an unprecedented time, our past and current choices affect how well we are able to handle the present trials and challenges. Our ability to endure or handle the unknowns of tomorrow reflects the depth and strength of our capacity, which is determined by the choices we've made in the past.

We make choices every day, whether we realize it or not, and they can affect our capacity negatively or positively. Our choices either increase or decrease our capacity. This is why our choices are the forerunners for rewards and consequences. None of us can escape the rewards or consequences of the choices we make. This underscores the importance of not letting bad people or circumstances influence us to make choices that might be detrimental to us and others within the sphere of our influence. Our choices have the capacity to put us and others in harm's way or to save us. Consequently, they can either open or close doors of opportunity for individuals and societies.

In all realms of life, the choices we make will be either advancing us, supporting us, enhancing us, or catapulting us into increase and affluences or decreasing us into retrogression, stagnation, and chaos, which might be detrimental to humanity. This is why choices are game changers in life's journey, because our choices determine the outcome of the changes that occur in our lives. The choices we make determine our capacity and resilience. They determine how far we soar in life, whether we are soaring, running, crawling, or struggling in any realm of life.

At every spot in life, when we are confronted with making a choice or choices, the choice we make eventually becomes our doorway or roadblock in that particular area of life, which can affect other areas of our lives. Our choices can either open doorways that allow us to get through certain situations, or they can create roadblocks in our lives that hinder our progress.

CHOICES DETERMINE CAPACITY

That is why our choices have the power to make us the victims of circumstance or the *crème de la crème* of society. They have the ability to position and reposition us in life and also to determine the outcome of any happenings in our lives. If we want to live a life of peace, joy, and influence, we most endeavor to make choices that will position us to achieve the status and stardom we desire in life. If peradventure we are not satisfied with the state of affairs in our lives, then we must make new choices that will reroute and reposition us individually or collectively along the right path.

The choices we make determine our capacity and results in life.

Choices Influence Capacity

The choices we make determine our capacity to handle things, and our capacity affects how mentally, emotionally, financially, and spiritually sufficient we are. Our sufficiency is always anchored on the choices we've made, which directly influence our capacity in all realms of life. Just as we cannot separate ourselves from our shadows, we cannot separate our choices from our capacity.

Building our capacity in any sphere of life begins with the choices we are making. Effectively, our choices either increase or decrease our capacity. Our ability to adapt, absorb, expand, or enlarge our capacity in different areas of life is orchestrated by the choices we make on a daily basis.

Our choices act as influencers and facilitators, as they determine the strength and depth of our capacity. Their effects can differ from situation to situation, but they are common denominators in the race of life.

When we apply the common denominators to our lives, they help us to increase and enlarge our capacity. For example, the following common denominators of our choices can increase our capacity:

- Acceptance of Responsibility

CHOICES ARE FORERUNNERS

- Acknowledgement of Weaknesses
- Being a Good Listener
- Being Sensitive
- Being Teachable
- Commitment
- Desiring to Excel
- Discipline
- Open Mindedness
- Personal Development
- Preparation
- Conscious of Time
- Willingness to Learn

All these are crucial in the Maze of Choices, because they influence the choices we make and directly influence our capacity in all realms of life. Nevertheless, it is vital for us to know that just as our choices influence our capacity in all spheres of life, our capacity also has the inherent power to influence our choices.

Capacity Influences Choice

It might be surprising to you to know that the choices we individually or collectively make or refuse to make not only influence our capacity but also our capacity has the power to influence the choices we make in all realms of life.

There are factors that enhance and undermine our capacity in different realms in life, and our capacity has the power to control the choices we make. In favorable and unfavorable conditions of life, the strength of our capacity influences the choices we make. It is also crucial to know that our capacity in one realm of life can have an across-the-board effect in other areas of our lives. For example:

CHOICES DETERMINE CAPACITY

- Our financial capacity influences the choices we make involving money. This controls all other areas of our lives and our dealings with others, which might differ from person to person.

- Our mental capacity influences all of our choices.

- Our physical capacity influences the choices we make around physical activities in our lives and what we dare to tackle in life.

- Our spiritual capacity influences the choices we make around spiritual things.

- Our social capacity reflects and affects our social performance in the society.

- Our sociological capacity influences the choices we make regarding the functioning of our society.

- Our learning capacity influences the choices we make regarding learning and concerning our open-mindedness.

- Our educational capacity influences the choices we make regarding our skills and expertise.

- Our managerial capacity influences the choices we make, which eventually determine our managerial performance.

- Our official capacity in the society influences the choices we make in each and every situation and in our response to events and activities.

Our capacity in all realms of life affects and controls the choices we make, which is directly reflected in our dealings because the choices we've made in the past have a way of interfering with the choices we make today. It's ironic that once we choose to develop our capacity in any sphere of life, the strength of our capacity in the given area becomes a governing factor that propels the private and public choices we make.

CHOICES ARE FORERUNNERS

Our strength and influence in any area of life reflects the depth of our capacity, while our capacity controls the choices we make in all situations. We must be mindful of this as life constantly throws a barrage of choices at us.

Barrage of Choices

We live our lives based on the choices that we make. Every day, as the sun rises and sets, we are bombarded with choices to make in one area of life or another: ranging from what to eat, drink, wear, what to do, what is a priority and what is not, where to go, the route we should take, who to call, how to respond to people, and other issues in our lives and more. These are just some of the choices that barrage us daily. The truth is, we consciously and subconsciously shape and mold our lives by the choices we make. It is quite fascinating to know that some of us are not aware of the fact that our realities are being orchestrated by the choices we make.

Our lives evolve and revolve around the choices we make daily. Our ability to choose correctly is being tested in every situation, and the results of such tests are seen in our lives and the transactions that transpire in our lives. These eventually make up our reality.

The rewards or consequences of the choices we make amid the barrage of choices might be instant or delayed. However, whether instant or delayed rewards or consequences, our outcomes in life are embedded in the choices we make in every area of life.

Our choices impact the results, experiences, and events that take place in our lives. Wherever we are in our lives today is the outcome of the choices we've made in the past, and the choices we make are our individual and collective investments to ourselves and others. That is why it is crucial to see beyond the present when making choices. Instead, we must have the future in mind, even when we are barraged with choices to make. It does not even matter if the choices that we are barraged with are trivial, profound, or significant.

All of them affect our future. Because the events and happenings of today are the successors of the choices we made yesterday, and the transactions that will transpire in our lives tomorrow will be the successors of the choices we make today. The choices we made yesterday are the predecessors of the experiences, happenings, and events that transpire in our lives today.

Our Choices Influence Our Future

The choices we make are like tools that create things. We can use our choices to create the future we desire. In all spheres of life, we knowingly and unknowingly use choices to create and decorate our futures. As such our choices eventually determine our outcomes and results in life. Our choices ultimately send either positive or negative signals to our environments, both our internal and external environments.

The choices we make on a daily basis have the power to create and influence our internal and external environments. Likewise, our internal and external environments are major propellers for our choices. Our ability to make the right choice depends on both our internal and external environments. The states of our internal and external environments are crucial in influencing our abilities to attain our goals and the futures we desire. In the Maze of Choices, our internal and external conditions influence our abilities to make right and good choices amid life challenges and situations.

Our internal and external environments propel us to create and decide our futures. Thus, our internal and external environments act as transmitters that control the series of events, happenings, or transactions that occur in our lives via the choices we make.

Our choices are always at the mercy of our internal and external environments. On the other hand, our internal and external environments are also at the mercy of our choices. Both our internal and external environments and the choices we make are dependent on each other and their interconnectedness influences our futures.

The Propulsion of Internal and External Conditions

In as much as choices create outcomes—they can send either negative or positive vibes to our environments—our choices are propelled by internal and external factors. Put in another way, our internal and external conditions influence our choices. When our internal or external conditions are not healthy, conducive, or favorable, then our choice will follow suit. Likewise, when our internal and external conditions are healthy, comfortable, and conducive to growth, we will certainly make better choices. The quality of our choices rely on our internal and external conditions.

Our interests in life are showcased in the choices we make; choices are reflective. Whatever we choose in any situation is a reflection of the choice we have made internally. Our behaviors, attitudes, and actions in any situation are channels we use to translate or transmit openly the choices we've made internally. It does not matter if we make impromptu choices or not. Our choices are made within and reflected outwardly by our actions.

Just as our internal and external conditions influence the choices we make, the choices we make also have the abilities to create, influence, and control our internal and external conditions. Likewise, our choices have the power to create internal and external issues, happenings, and situations in our lives, which might be favorable or unfavorable to us; that is how strong the power of choice is in our lives. Our ability to choose correctly in any situation depends on both our internal and external conditions. Although, both internal and external factors might act as propellers for our choices, ultimately, we are solely responsible for the choices we make.

We Are Responsible for Our Choices

Life is lived based on the choices we make daily. At the same time, people we encounter in our lives affect how we make choices. Nevertheless, at the end of the day, we are responsible for the choices we've made, and we should take ownership of them. Although the influences of others in our lives can have a tremendous impact on us, we are the ones who eventually make our choices. The choices we make are ours irrespective of the external influences, such as human personalities or circumstantial factors that compel us to make these choices. We are solely responsible for our choices.

Sometimes, situations and people might pressurize us, individually or collectively as a group, into making choices, which might create negative or positive outcomes. It is crucial to always remember that our choices don't affect us alone but may affect others who are vulnerable around us. Our choices always create something in our lives and in the lives of those around us. Choices are like a splash of water that falls on everyone who is in the cascading pathway of the choices made.

Our Choices Are Reflective

Our choices are reflective, they reflect back on every facet of our lives. Every choice we make can be seen in our actions, words, and dealings. When we make a choice internally and act on it externally, our actions and words reflect our internal choice. After we make a choice and act on it, that choice becomes an active force in our lives, which can eventually set, in motion a chain reaction that can initiate good or bad changes in our lives and in the lives of others.

The reflection of our choices in our lives can be seen in the happenings, events, and transactions that transpire in our lives and in the lives of those around us. Whether we make choices privately or publicly, the truth is our choices always have a way of catching up with us. This is because our choices always beam a ray of light on us that is translucent for all to seen without our permission. The events, happenings, and transactions that transpire in our lives are the reflections of the choices we've made in the past and the choices we are making now.

Active and Passive Actions

In the Maze of Choices, action is a major stakeholder in initiating the choices we make. Actions can be active or passive. An active action is the act of taking action and acting on the choice that we make, whereas the passive action is the opposite.

A passive action is the act of not acting or doing something about the choice that was made. It is the act of passively collaborating with whatever might transpire. Although it might be a passive action, it has the power to produce an outcome, which might not be what we originally desired. Both active and passive actions have the power to birth an outcome in our lives; however, most of us are not aware of the power of active and passive actions, especially as they relate to initiating change in our lives.

It is crucial to note that actions, whether active or passive, have the power to influence and set the choice wheels in motion, because not taking an action is an action in and of itself. Actions are the instruments that stir and activate every choice, and active and passive actions have the power to interfere with our choice.

Active, Inactive, and Dormant Choices

In life, the choices we make can be classified as active, inactive, and dormant. Each of these types of choice has the power to produce different outcomes in our lives, and any of these types can directly or indirectly influence, impact, and impede our lives and environments.

These types can each be defined as follows:

- **Active choices**: These are choices that are acted upon. A choice or choices become active when the force of action is applied to trigger them. Action is applied to activate the choice, which in turn initiates a process that will eventually produce an outcome. The resulting outcome can be positive or negative, depending on what the choice originally entails. The difference between active and inactive choices is the application of the force of action as it pertains to active choices. Any choice made without action makes the choice inactive.

- **Inactive choices:** These are choices that we make but which we do not act on. In this case, the choices have been made but the force of action was not applied to activate the choices. However, not applying the force of action to trigger a choice made does not necessarily mean that the choice made doesn't have the power to produce a reward or consequence. The truth is, even inactive choices have the inherent power to affect lives. However, inactive choices can be temporarily or permanently in an inactive mode. Most of the time, procrastination is a major component of inactive choices, and procrastination can be a weapon we use individually or collectively to make a choice inactive.

- **Dormant choices:** These are choices that should have been made but were not made; hence, they remain dormant. Sometimes, some dormant choices are vital and crucial to our survival as humans. Dormant choices are sometimes vehemently ignored or suspended due to reasons or excuses that vary from one situation and individual to another. However, the refusal to make a choice does not weaken the strength of the choice; neither will it stop the outcome because, as we have seen, not making a choice is a choice in and of itself. Dormant choices have the power to start a process and produce an outcome without our permission.

Active, inactive, or dormant types of choices have the inherent power to produce an outcome in our lives as individuals and in the lives of our families, communities, and our society.

Active, inactive, and dormant choices have the power to produce both negative and positive outcomes in our lives, and acting or not acting on our choices has the power to produce results with or without our consent. Therefore, active, inactive, and dormant choices are the facilitators of all actions and reactions in the streets of life.

Our choices and decisions are activated by actions. These actions cause reactions which eventually lead to rewards or consequences. Sometimes, we are not ready to face or accept the consequences that our choices create.

Choice Equations

There are different calculations and equations that are consciously and subconsciously being solved as we journey through life. At one point or another, we all have been engaged in solving one or more of these equations in our lives.

Choice => Decision => Action => Reaction => Results => Reward or Consequence

C => D => A => R => R => R or C

Choice => Decision => Procrastination => No Action => Reaction => Results => No Reward or Consequence

C => D => P => N A => R => R => N-R or C

Choice => Decision =>Ignore/Suspend =>Reaction => Results => Positive or Negative

C => D => I/S => R => R => P or N

In every sphere of life, active choices are more profitable, especially when the choice is geared toward profitable goals. However, in life, the inactive and dormant choices can have their own advantages and disadvantages. Our actions, attitudes, behavior, interests, values, and responses to situations and people showcase our choices in any particular situation.

CHOICES DETERMINE CAPACITY

The place of choice—whether active, inactive, or dormant—is the fertilization of decision. By the same token, action, procrastination, and suspense are the catalysts for executing or hindering our choices.

Our choices are the raw material for making decisions while actions, procrastination, or suspension are the forces that process our decisions and that trigger a reaction which creates results. In the end, these results are called rewards or consequences, and they represent the end of the choice circle.

> **Rewards and consequences are the highlights of the choices we make.**

CHAPTER 3

CHOICES HAVE REWARDS OR CONSEQUENCES

CHOICES ALWAYS COME with rewards and consequences. Rewards and consequences are the outcomes of our choices. When our choices are bad, the consequences become, a shadow that sticks with us individually or collectively, and sometimes for the rest of our lives. If our choices are good, then the reward becomes a stepping-stone that helps us to make progress in the race of life.

Whatever we become is enforced by the power of the choices we made. In life's journey, our choices produce different substances and things, which comes in different forms and which are translated into our lives as consequences and rewards. The choices we make plugs us into different lifelines in all areas of life. The choices we make determine the altitude we fly and operate in during different phases of life. In all realms of life, our choices always align with our desires, which are most times the propellers of the choices we make. Our choices draw the pattern, which eventually creates and forms our lifestyles. That is how choices conceive the events that transpire in our lives.

CHOICES ARE FORERUNNERS

Not all choices are revisable or revocable. Once a choice has been made and activated by action, it can be difficult to undo it, especially if someone's welfare is on the line. Opportunities might arise to amend our choices; however, we can never totally erase their consequences. Forgiveness and healing might take place, but the scars of bad choice or choices made will remain; while the benefit or reward of the good choice made blossoms and produces fruits that benefit everyone concerned.

Our choices are like seed that we plant for a future harvest. All of our choices produce some kind of fruit in our lives and sometimes in the lives of others. That is why we must be conscious and intentional about the choices we make in order for them to be a blessing to us and to others.

Choices are seeds that we sow both in our lives and in the lives of others. Eventually the harvest arrives where we will eat the fruit of our choices. This circle is set in motion once the sowing has been done.

Our choices are like seeds that we sow into our future and sometimes into the future of others as well.

Choices Are Like Seeds

Each of us carries around a bag full of different seeds called choices. These "seeds" shape, control, and influence all aspects of our lives.

As we go about our various endeavors and activities, we are continually confronted with opportunities to choose. As we choose, we unseemly sow the seeds of our choices in different areas of life as we wish. We consciously and subconsciously sow the seeds of our choices into the soils of our lives and into the lives of others. Our choices eventually take root downward and produce branches bearing fruits known as rewards and consequences. These branches can become either nuisances that create discomfort or a welcome shade that protects us from the blazes of life's sun.

CHOICES HAVE REWARDS OR CONSEQUENCES

Choices, just like seeds have the inherent power to produce. Rewards and consequences are the end products or fruits of the choices we sow. In every sphere of life, we are responsible to choose the choice seeds that we want to sow. Unfortunately, we do not have the absolute power to always know what kind of fruit our choices will bear come harvest season. The magnitude of our success in any area of life is determined by the choice seeds we sow. Our choices determine how we will live our lives and the harvest we reap in life.

Each and every one of us has been given the solemn power to choose and to make choices in the affairs of our lives and sometimes in the affairs of others, based on the position or office we are privileged to occupy. The products or outcomes of our choices become our harvest in due season, for better or for worse.

There is always a due season when our choices become our realities.

The Due Season of Choices

There is a due season to produce an outcome for every activity under the sun, and in life, there are due seasons for our choices. It is imperative to know that once our choices have been set in motion, there is a set time for them to produce outcomes.

The outcome of our choices eventually becomes our reality. Just as we have expiration dates printed on different products, choices have expiration dates known as their due season. *Due season* is the set time when each and every one of us will reap the outcome of our choices as harvests in our lives.

The truth is, most of us are not conscious of the fact that there is a due season for our choices. Nevertheless, whether we are aware of that fact or not, each of our choices has a due season when they become real in our lives as our experiences and stories.

When we make a choice, we have the power to choose the choice seed we want to sow. However, we do not have the absolute power to determine what they will produce.

The Harvest of Choices

We all know that there is something in a seed that bears fruit. Our choices are like seeds, which will definitely produce *fruits* in our lives. Our choices have the ability to produce multiple fruits in terms of results, outcomes, or experiences in our lives. Sometimes they also produce fruits in the lives of others as well. The harvest or outcomes of our choices can result in a chain reaction, which will eventually have a domino effect we might not be able to control or stop until it runs its full course.

Different choices will produce different kinds of fruit. For instance, when a person continuously makes poor, wrong, or illicit choices, their harvest will be poor and deformed. Conversely, impactful and empowering choices result in bumper harvests filled with positive impact and empowerment.

When we make deficient choices, the harvest of such choices will be deficient. When a person chooses to defame others, he or she will certainly reap a defamatory harvest. Remember, whatever we sow we also reap; that is the fact of life.

Our choices initiate a process that produces substances in our lives, which become our harvests. When we make choices in any area of life, in the end, we and others either pay the price for the poor, bad, and wrong choices made, or we reap the good harvest based on good choices.

This is the truth and the reality of the freedom to choose. One way or another, the choice seeds we sow in our lives and in the lives of others always yield harvests. These harvests can transcend into our future to help, empower, enhance, propel, and promote us, or they

CHOICES HAVE REWARDS OR CONSEQUENCES

can hinder, impede, stagnate, and frustrate us or create anarchy in our lives and in the lives of others.

Our choices create experiences and outcomes. They have the power to change any situation and circumstance.

Below are examples of choice seeds and their resulting harvests:

Choice Seed Sown	Resulting Harvest
Acceptance	Unity
Preparation	Opportunity
Opportunity	Access
Dedication	Recognition
Focus	Results
Applied Knowledge	Enlarged Capacity
Inspiration	Creativity
Love	Peace and Unity
Grace	Favor
Respect	Honor
Nurturing	Empowerment
Investment	Relationship and Rewards
Taking Responsibility	Territorial Dominion
Dedication	Outstanding Results
Friendship	Support
Solidarity	Unity
Input	Result
Dispute	War
War	Anarchy
Gossip	Enmity
Discrimination	Segregation
Irritation	Anger

CHOICES ARE FORERUNNERS

Discord	Strife
Mistake and Error	Shame
Bullying	Victim
Rejection	Depression

Our outcomes or results in life can be traced back to the choice seeds that we sow. Therefore, whatever our choices entail determines the outcomes we will experience (rewards or punishments).

The application of useful knowledge is the baseline for good, just and smart choices whereas ignorance is the baseline for poor and wrong choices.

Good, Right, Bad, Poor, and Wrong Choices

The choices we make in any sphere of life can be good, right, bad, wrong, or poor choices. The truth is, at one point or another, all of us have been involved in making one of these kinds of choices. Some of these choices we are proud of and some we regret. In all of our endeavors, our experiences, outcomes, and results serve to validate if our choices are good, right, just, smart, bad, poor, or wrong.

Pain, sorrow, suffering, and regret are the wages of bad choices.

Bad Choices

Bad choices invoke disastrous consequences and outcomes. Most bad choices hurt or harm others. In the Maze of Choices, the wages of bad choices are bad outcomes that might lead to sorrow, setbacks, and regrets.

Sometimes, we unconsciously make ourselves and others voluntary victims of circumstances because of the poor and bad choices we make.

Regrets, shame, and pain are the companions of bad choices most of the time. In a nutshell, bad choices never travel alone. They are always accompanied and surrounded with companions which we might not want to accommodate in our lives.

Bad choices are triggered by external and internal influences, such as associations, our environment, our emotions and mindsets, etc. Most bad choices are anchored on ignorance, and ignorance is the baseline for acting or choosing foolishly. This can lead us to make irrational choices, which become the breeding ground for more bad choices in the future.

Just because a choice is wrong, does not necessarily mean it's bad. Sometimes it just simply isn't the best option available for a given situation.

Wrong Choices

Wrong choices are unsuitable and incorrect choices concerning a particular situation. We often make these choices out of ignorance or because we are inadequately informed. Just because a choice is wrong, does not necessarily mean it is bad. Sometimes it is not the best option for a given situation, or the timing is not right.

Most wrong choices are like wolves in a sheep's clothing, and ignorance, misinterpretations, and assumptions are all major sponsors of most wrong choices. We must endeavor to equip ourselves adequately with the necessary information before making choices. This goes for all choices including trivial, profound, or significant choices.

Wisdom is the foundation of all good and right choices.

Right Choices

Right choices are choices that are just and suitable for their circumstances. They might not necessarily be the best choice or option, but they might be the right choice to make due to the circumstances.

CHOICES ARE FORERUNNERS

Sometimes, it is not easy to make right choices amid difficult situations, but when it is ethically and morally beneficial to do so, they become just and honorable choices to make. In life-threatening situations, right choices are compensations for the prevailing circumstances in order to rescue and save lives and properties.

Right choices set things in order. They produce positive outcomes and results. Right choices amid challenging situations of life might not be the best choices at face value; however, they are always the best route to take to keep us afloat amid the storms of life. Right choices are tailored to handle and confront issues. Sometimes, right choices are simply the survival choice, which is crucial for resolving confrontations.

Amid the challenges of life, every right choice has the power to resolve, restore, and reshape situations, even when the previous choices yielded unpleasant outcomes. Right choices are like a reverse gear that reroutes us from confronting challenges to solving challenges, which is more profitable and productive. Right choices have the inherent power to redirect, reroute, and guide us to the right paths. They help us to find solutions to life's issues.

Good choices enhance our value and empower us.

Good Choices

Good choices are the best choices we can make in any given situation. Good choices are wisely chosen out of the vast amount, of available options to choose from in any given situation or circumstance. It is the choice that has the desired qualities or attributes necessary to produce a satisfactory outcome that will be beneficial to all parties involved. Good choices enhance our value and empower us. They are always efficient and reliable in producing virtuous and fruitful outcomes.

Whatever choices we make regarding the different affairs of our lives, it is vital to be conscious of the fact that the choices we make also serve as emissaries in our lives and as the building blocks we use to construct our lives.

Our choices reflect our values, mindset, and moral standards.

Choices Are Emissaries

Our choices are like emissaries that are deployed into the future. They help prepare the way for us and also convey our interests, desires, goals, values, morals and mindsets. This eventually propels us and enforces the outcome in life's endeavors. Our choices broadcast our values, mindsets, and ethics.

What is more, our choices are not only our emissaries but also our building blocks which we use daily to build and lay foundations in different areas of our lives. Our choices lay the foundation from which all our life's endeavors are launched.

Choices propel all of the transactions in the streets of life. Our choices are the catalysts of all actions and reactions, which create the situations and events that transpire in our lives. In all endeavors of life, our choices act as our representatives. They set the pace for the possibilities and opportunities that comes our way.

All activities on earth revolve around choices. Our choices determine the path we take in life.

Our Choices Reveal Content

Our choices are incubated internally before being revealed externally in the form of actions and subsequent reactions. The outcome can be rewarding or consequential.

Our choices reveal content and our thought patterns. In every situation, the choice we make reveals our mentalities, emotions, will, and thoughts regarding any given situation. Our content, which is our internal environment, is the generating force that corresponds with our external environment to propel our choices forward. Content is expressed through our choices, which are communicated through our actions. Our outcomes and experiences point directly back to our choices.

The choices we make reveal our content and the state of our internal environment. They include our emotional, mental, or spiritual environments. In the Maze of Choices, the state of our internal environment, (our content) is transmitted via the choices we make. Our content is a constant motivator that propels our choices forward.

Choices Are Transmitted through Different Channels

We will continue to make choices for as long as we are alive. Our choices are transmitted through different channels. Below are some of the channels:

- Attitude
- Behavior
- Energy
- Input
- Interest
- Morals
- Resources
- Response
- Result
- Time
- Values
- Words

CHOICES HAVE REWARDS OR CONSEQUENCES

Whatever channel we choose to transmit our choices, the choices we make today do not just disappear. Rather, they go ahead of us into our future to produce the inevitable or instigate a new process or circle that might be profitable or detrimental. The choices we make today will certainly show up in our future, in one form or another, to stir up an eventuality in our lives. These eventualities can cause, ignite, or inflame issues and events. In any situation, in spite of our emotions, circumstances, or desires, it is mandatory to engage and have the picture of the future we want before making any choice. This matters even regarding choices we think are trivial.

Engaging the Future through Choices

In life, there is always a way that seems right to a man, but the end thereof is destruction. Likewise, there are choices that might seem right to us but sometimes the end of such choices can be hurtful, harmful, or destructive.

This is the dicey side of choice-making. It becomes crucial to engage the future and carefully consider the possible outcome before making any choice.

We need to evaluate our past choices and not to fall into the same pit holes of poor, bad, and wrong choices. The choices we make today align us with our tomorrow. Today's choices serve as preview and prophecy of our future.

Choices precede success or failure in life.

The outcomes of our lives mirror the choices we make. Nothing can separate our results in life from the choices we have made. Our choices precede success or failure in life.

Since choices precede success or failure, we must carefully weigh all options available before we make a choice. Making choices this way can help us to avert mishaps in the future. This is because the choice that might seem to be good or right now might be bad tomorrow.

CHOICES ARE FORERUNNERS

We should not make choices within the span of the moment; rather we should consider the future when we make choices. Remember, choices are like seeds. What we plant now we will reap later.

Our past choices might seem like they were the best choices at the time, but in hindsight we can sometimes realize they were pitfalls because we did not consider the future. Engaging and exploiting the future by having a futuristic approach in making choices will help us to make better choices. When the future is not engaged in our choice-making, a negative wheel might be set in motion, which when not stopped or halted in time, it can result in an adverse outcome.

The choices we make every day have the power to make us lose the beautiful memories of yesterday and the great opportunities and possibilities of tomorrow.

Rewards and Punishments Are the Outcome of Choices

The choices we make always produce something in our lives, which can come in the form of a reward or punishment. All the events that transpire in our lives are there to either reward us or punish us.

Our present reality reflects our previous choices. Our accolades and affluence are the result of our past choices. Conversely, our shame and regret are the punishments of poor, bad, and illicit choices from our past. Ultimately, rewards or consequences become the forerunners of all the events and happenings that will comprise our lives. Those rewards or punishments are anchored to our choices.

> The currents that are embedded in our choices diffuse into our lives. As they do, they create energy waves that either brighten or send shock waves through our lives.

CHAPTER 4

THE CHOICE METER

CHOICES CONTROL AND direct our lives. The choices we make in different spheres of our lives are measured by what I call a "Choice Meter." The choice meter reads, calculates, and cumulates the outcomes, eventualities, and happenings of our choices. The Choice Meter is anything that shows, reflects, and translates our choices into our realities.

These realities can be positive or negative, uplifting or downgrading, appeasing or aggravating, depending on the reading on the Choice Meter. The choices we make can be a highway of empowerment, embedded with possibilities for success or failure. Choices are the vehicle we use to navigate through every state of life. Choices are our mode of transportation. They bring each of us to our various destinations throughout our lives.

Our speed and velocity in any area of life are controlled and measured by our choices. The Choice Meter is what measures and gauges the outcomes of every choice we make. It shows us how our choices manifest themselves in our lives and in the lives of others.

Readings on the Choice Meter can be weak or strong. Weak readings are illicit, bad, or poor choices, while strong readings are the good, right, or just choices. Regardless of the strength of our choices, they all have the power to impact us and others. Whatever the reading, one thing is certain, our choices initiate changes in our lives. The gravity of those changes is determined by what the choices entail, including the process used to make them.

Choice Meter Readings

Most of the activities and transactions in life are measured in one way or another. These measurements take place in different areas of our lives, such as our education, skills, career, and relationships. In all realms of life, there is a visible and invisible measuring gauge that is measuring our progress, performance, and achievements.

The Choice Meter measures the effects, impacts, and the shock waves that our choices make in our lives and in the lives of others. The choices we make in different areas of our lives are monitored and measured on a daily basis. This happens with or without our consent. Eventually, the readings become our realities.

The readings and their outcomes create a baseline for our daily lives. Sadly, many are not aware of this. Choice Meter readings differ from person to person and from situations to situations. The readings on the Choice Meter vary because each of us makes different choices, even if we are given the same situations.

The Choice Meter reflects every outcome and happening in our life. The Choice Meter sums up our choices in life when the Choice Cycle is completed. Its readings can be seen in the activities and transactions in our lives. All careers, professions, relationships, business dealings, transactions, conversations, and decisions reflect the outcomes of the readings of the Choice Meter.

The Choice Meter tells and reflects the options we have chosen in a given situation. The options which we have chosen consciously, subconsciously, or intentionally are then seen publicly in the fruits of our endeavors once the Choice Cycle has been completed.

Choice Cycle

Every choice has a timeframe in which to produce an outcome. The duration can vary from one choice to another. The effects and the changes each choice initiates might differ from one choice to another. Ultimately, every choice has a time frame that it follows before it yields an outcome. This is especially true when the Choice Wheel has been set in motion. Just as we have a billing cycle in different business transactions that take place in the streets of life, there is also a Choice Cycle that yields outcomes in our life.

The billing cycle kicks in once a choice completes the Choice Circle. The Choice Meter's readings determine the charges or benefits due from the billing cycle which are translated as outcomes, events, or happenings in our lives. These outcomes, events, or happenings trigger different things in our lives depending on what our choices are. However, the charges and benefits eventually become life experiences.

> **Be not deceived, bad choices corrupt and puncture future opportunities.**

The Life Highway

Our choices determine the paths we take in life. They determine and control the duration, speed, flexibility, peace, smoothness, or roughness of every endeavor we undertake in life. Sometimes, our choices create a highway or an unpaved road in our life. Choices determine how smooth or rough our journey through life will be.

When a highway is broad and smooth it attracts traffic, but when a road is unpaved and filled with potholes, most of the time, commuters try as much as possible to avoid it, especially when there are better options available. That's how our choices are. Good choices attract people (traffic), but bad choices divert people away from the person who makes poor choices. Whatever road we find ourselves on in life's journey can be traced back to our choices, and our past choices can negatively impact the traffic of opportunities, honor, favor and possibilities that flow through our lives. Just as good and well-connected highways attract a lot of commuters and motorists, our choices determine what we attract into our lives.

The choices we make in life have the power to either commission or decommission us at one point or the other. The choices we make have the power to make room for us in the pinnacle of our endeavors and bring us before great men.

Choices Controls Traffic

The choices we make, control and determine the good and bad traffic in our lives. Choices orchestrate the flow and transit of people and things in our lives. Our choices act as traffic controllers and they determine the events and happenings in our lives, and our choices can attract or cut off good or viable opportunities.

Our choices determine the routes we take in life. Good, positive, and profitable choices attract an inflow of traffic, especially when they carry an idea that will be profitable to humanity; but bad, negative, and unprofitable choices block traffic, opportunities, possibilities, and influences. In the end, our choices determine the climates and aura around us and the experiences we attract into our lives.

Our choices create entrances in our lives and experiences of other that are like pathways, which allow us to access possibilities, opportunities, and experiences. In every aspect of life, our choices are the doorway to honor, dignity, and good health; however, they can also lead to shame, regret, reproach, and stagnation.

This is how powerful our choices are—through our choices we influence our positioning in the race of life. When we desire to live a life of honor, respect, dignity, or affluence, our choices determine if these desires will become a reality in our lives. On the flip side, mediocrity stems from our choices. Our choices either empower us to go forward and succeed in life, or they pull us back and derail us from success.

Choices Can Elevate, Direct, or Derail

The Maze of Choice is the place where we decide what our life outcomes will be. Our choices always produce outcomes. These can elevate, direct, or derail us. Good choices direct and elevate us towards a path of possibilities. They make opportunities accessible to our lives. Only good and right choices have the power to elevate us to greater heights, while bad and poor choices derail us and lead us off course.

Our choices are the forerunners, vanguard, and rearguard of all of our transactions. Our choices bind together all the things we do in life. The outcomes of our choices always create waves that can elevate, empower, inspire, or even derail us and others. These waves can be transmitted into our lives and the lives of others around us, with or without their permission, because choices carry in them a current that is transmittable.

> ***Our choices create magnetic fields around us that ensure their fulfillment.***

The Current of Choice

Our choices are not only reflective, they, also carry with them a magnetic force which attracts and repels what flows through our lives. Our choices form a current that flows through our life and through the lives of others. These currents transport different things into our lives and into the lives of others, such as tangible or intangible substances. These substances come in the form of happenings and events. Just as electricity carries different types of transmittable currents, likewise, our choices carry currents which are continuously transmitted into different areas of our lives and into the lives of others.

CHOICES ARE FORERUNNERS

Whatever current our choices carry they eventually determine our experiences in life. The current that flows through the choices we make can be a positive, negative, or neutral current. Each of these are translated into different happenings. The happenings then are transmitted and expressed in our life as good or bad, profitable or unprofitable outcomes.

Tracking statistics of our life's events enables us to identify whether our choices are operating at high or low voltage. The voltage of the current that flows through our choices determines the frequency of our success, victory, or defeat in any spheres of life. The impact of our choices depends on the type of current and velocity that it carries. However, the velocity and volatility of our choices differs from one person to another.

The velocity and volatility of choices varies depending on your status in life. For instance, the choices of a clerk and a president differ in strength and impact. It is crucial to be conscious of the reality that our choices carry currents. These currents are transmitted into different areas of our lives and into the lives of others, and they can create either an equilibrium or an imbalance in our lives.

> *Just as we were not created to walk alone in life, our choices do not walk alone. The choices we make have the power to attract more choices, as such they never walk alone.*

CHAPTER 5

COMMON GROUNDS

WE ALL MAKE different choices. Irrespective of our age, race, gender, skills, talents, education, or status, choices are as essential for our existence as oxygen. They are crucial for our existence as humans. The Maze of Choices is where we as humans meet and interact although the choices we make might differ from person to person. Nevertheless, there are certain areas of life where we have to make choices which are common to us all.

The choices we make in these common grounds eventually determine the activities and transactions that transpire in our lives. Our choices initiate most of what happens in our future. The common ground of our choices is where our choices as humans are interwoven and connected to each other. It is where they orchestrate and set the ball rolling for different events in our lives. At a certain point in life, everyone makes a choice from the common ground of choices. Still, the outcomes are always different for each of us.

The choices we make in the common ground of choices are projected into our futures, and they predict the course and direction of our lives. Simply put, the choices we make today give us a preview of our future. Our choices lay a foundation onto which other choices are laid. Our choices are front runners, presenters, and masters of ceremony; they hail and beckon other choices. Our choices trigger chain reactions that lead to subsequent choices. This can be profitable or unprofitable for us depending on the content of the choices

Different Types of Common Ground

Attitude: Attitudes are the expression of one's emotions, mentality, and opinions. They are consciously chosen, and they reflect our choices concerning people, issues, or situations. At different points in life, we all exhibit one type of attitude or another. We exhibit different attitudes as a way to express our choices.

Attitudes are expressed in different dimensions and are constantly and actively exhibited across all of the spectrums of our lives. They include thankfulness, gratitude, appreciation, contentment, encouragement, complaining, ingratitude, arrogance, snobbishness, and entitlement. Attitude is also a common ground in the Maze of Choices since we have the freedom to choose the attitude we want to exhibit at any given time. Our attitudes express the choices that we make internally.

Our attitudes differ depending on the situation and on our experience, perception, and interpretation of situations and circumstances. Our choices reflect the path we choose, and the path is transmitted by our attitude(s). Our body language, responses, and reactions to situations reflect our attitudes. It is important to realize that these reactions impact the atmosphere around us. Our attitudes have the power to appease and pacify situations in our favor. They can also aggravate or provoke a chain reaction that can result in negative outcomes to situations.

Change: At different times of life, we all desire something to change in our lives. We might want a change in our finances, relationships, career, status, lifestyle, or performance. We also tend to resist change and are often not willing to embrace any alteration or modification to our habits or lifestyle. Changes always involve alterations to our way of life. They also sometimes make us get out of our comfort zones and can cause discomfort in our lives.

Changes can accelerate things in our lives or put the brakes on them. They can also reverse things in our lives. Overall change is vital for our lives because it can reorient us or help speed us up towards our goals. As humans, we cannot escape change, even when we try to resist it. Changes are inevitable. As a result, our ability to reach new heights in life is determined by our willingness to embrace change.

Effort: There are situations in everyone's life where we have to choose and make effort to go the extra mile. Effort is essential in life. To attain a goal, we often have to go the extra mile. We often have to compel ourselves to tackle a difficult task that might be an obstacle to our goals.

Effort means that we consciously and intentionally choose to bring life and energy into our lives and endeavors. Putting forth effort means we make a calculated choice meant to engage force onto our life. It means that we set our minds on something and raise the bar. We set out a target and become driven to reach it, that's effort. All humans desire to push themselves to a better place in life. Whether we are aware of it or not, we directly or indirectly put effort into our endeavors.

Effort means that we choose not to give up or give in to prevailing circumstances in our lives. These circumstances might vary or differ from one person to another but the desire not to give up or give in is common to us all. Effort brings us stamina and helps us press on. It brings a boost to our system and life so we can keep on going.

At one point or another in the race of life, we will be compelled by life challenges to make the choice to go the extra mile in order to achieve our heart's desire. In such cases, self-encouragement is crucial because we don't always have people to cheer us on. Effort keeps us from quitting, and it helps us push on until we reach the finish line with or without the encouragement of others.

Laid-Back: There are times in life when we just need to let go for different reasons. When we take a laid-back approach individually or collectively, we make a choice not to tackle or address a situation or issue. Sometimes we choose to not be worried or anxious about a situation that might need urgent attention in our lives, and as such, we treat urgent things casually.

A laid-back approach means that we go through stages of life with a carefree attitude. We thus make no attempt to empower, invest, upgrade, or enhance our lives, even if an opportunity presents itself. It's a nonchalant choice that is synonymous with an "I don't care" mentality or an "I will do it later" mindset.

We are all laid-back at one time or another. However, there are people who permanently take up a laid-back mode of life. They respond in a laid-back manner to both the trivial and the important matters of life. In the Maze of Choices, every laid-back choice we make as humans can be seen in our lives and endeavors. Therefore, when we choose to engage in a laid-back mentality, the results and outcomes will show.

Re-evaluating: There comes a time in life when each and every one of us will step aside from the busyness of our schedules to re-evaluate our lives. These reflective moments of re-evaluation often trigger in us a desire for change. This desire can create a vacuum that cannot be filled until changes that we deem necessary take place in our lives.

In the race of life, dissatisfaction triggers a search for fulfillment, which initiates the need to re-evaluate our choices. Our dissatisfaction triggers a yearning in us, and this yearning initiates a desire for improvement, which becomes the driving force that controls our choices

All humans experience discontentment at one point or another. It compels us to evaluate our choices. Whenever we accept the outcome of our evaluation and make the necessary changes, we enhance our lives, and we find out that our lives have been rerouted and redirected.

When we choose to improve ourselves, we open ourselves up to new possibilities and opportunities.

Improvement: Improvement takes place when an individual, community, or organization chooses to improve themselves. Improvement means that we make a concerted effort to be better today than we were yesterday. It helps us progress through life.

This choice is usually triggered by not being satisfied or content with the status quo of our everyday life. It creates in us a hunger and a yearning for more. It happens when we feel a sense of inner conviction that life can be better than the way it is now.

It helps us stretch our capacity and in turn lends to our self-improvement. When we want to improve ourselves, we choose to be a blessing to ourselves and to others

Inspiration: Everyone depends on God, others, and the environment for inspiration. When we are inspired, we can attain new heights in our various endeavors. We are often inspired by the success of others who are role models in our lives. Their lives serve as a road map for us, which stimulates and motivates us to succeed. All of us have imitated others at one time or another in order to succeed at something we enjoy. In fact, we often emulate those we look up to and follow in their footsteps.

We need to be inspired in all seasons of life. This means being inspired during times that are joyful, difficult, challenging, and even distressing. All of us need someone to inspire, stimulate, and motivate us to continue on the right path. In the end, inspiration enables us to achieve our goals and dreams.

Inspirational choices equip and empower us to succeed and to keep on going in the midst of challenges. It is important to note that those who benefit from inspiration are those who are willing to be inspired by the success, words of wisdom, and discipline of others.

CHOICES ARE FORERUNNERS

Time: Time is crucial for our existence. Human life is measured in time. This is why humans celebrate birthdays and other milestones. Time is intertwined with our existence on earth. Just as time cannot be separated from our lives, no man can live without making choices.

All human activities on earth revolves around time. We have all been allocated an equal amount of time each day. It does not matter if we are rich or poor, educated or uneducated, wise or ignorant. We all get 24 hours per day to go about our business. However, what differentiates one person from another are the choices that we make regarding how we utilize our time and how well we engage the time at our disposal.

How we utilize our time matters. Most, if not all, of our choices are constrained by time. Our choices are stipulated and controlled by time. Hence choices are time oriented. Time oriented choices are choices that need to be made within a certain frame of time because of their urgency. Our refusal to make a choice on time or by an appropriate time might result in consequences. These can have minor or severe effects.

Time oriented choices are choices that are controlled by time. I refer to them as *Timely Choices*. Not utilizing time wisely can negatively affect our lives. Our choices often relate to time in the following ways:

> *Rewards*—All of our transactions in life are time oriented. Every opportunity in the streets of life is framed and governed by time. Choices that engender rewards are those that are made at an appropriate time. In the Maze of Choices, it is our recognition of our hour of visitation by life opportunities and possibilities in any sphere of life that make it a reality. Our ability to discern and know the perfect time to make certain choice in life births rewards and satisfactions in many areas of life.
>
> *Minor Consequences*—Minor consequences occur as a result of not making choices at an appropriate time. These

choices can trigger setbacks in areas of life where we don't make choices at the appropriate time. Thankfully, the consequences might not always be grievous because we might still have the possibility to rectify or amend the faults or errors of our choices. In spite of setbacks or temporary halts in our progress there might still be a glimpse of hope because the window of time might not be fully closed yet. Still, such choices stifle our progress since we did not make the right choice to begin with (when the timing was appropriate).

Severe Consequences—There is time for everything under heaven. In life, there is time to make certain choices. Our refusal to make right choices when we need to can result in grievous outcomes. These can be severe and devastating to our lives, which is why they are called severe consequences.

Many times, untimely choices leave wounds that cannot heal and that mar the lives of individuals, families, communities, organizations, and even countries. For example, governmental choices can derail lives, trigger war, and cause crises which can lead to devastating outcomes. Likewise, when someone refuses to cherish and tell those close to them how much they love them before passing on, it can leave vacuum that cannot be filled.

There comes a time in the lives of each and every one of us when the power to choose will no longer be at our disposal. This is why we all have to make haste while we are still alive. Choices are constrained by time and all human beings have a limited amount of time to fulfil their purpose and destiny here on earth.

Since we are limited by time, we must be mindful of the choices we make.

Choices Are Time Oriented: As human beings, there are areas of life where we all have to make choices which are common to all of us. Some of these choices are time oriented and once the window of time closes, we will face the consequences of our choices. We must align our choices with time because all things are not possible all the time. That is why there are times and seasons for all the activities under the sun.

There are certain choices in life that are time oriented and these choices must be made within a stipulated time frame. Any attempt to ignore the stipulated window of time can and will result in minor or grievous outcomes. Also, once a window closes, we aren't always able to change the choices we made.

While you might be living in an era of grace, there can come a time in your life when that time might pass. The choices you refuse to make then become irrevocable. This is what it means for choices to be time oriented.

Choices are time oriented because grace will no longer work for us if we refuse to use the window of time that was opened to us. We don't have forever to honor, love, and respect our parents. We must do all of those while they are still alive. You must love, cherish, and invest time with your children or spouse. You must appreciate and respect people, and above all you must say the prayer of salvation while there is still time left.

Once the stipulated time frame closes, it will be impossible for you to make a different choice. This is why it is crucial for us to know that some choices in life cannot be pushed aside or postponed.

Time Is Invaluable

All activities under the sun are time oriented and programmed within a specified frame of time. There is nothing we do that is not governed by or at the mercy of time. Time is an imperative factor that relates to our choices. It is essential to consider time when we make choices because all of the activities in our lives are governed by time.

Every purpose in life is time oriented, and time governs all the transactions and purpose in the streets of life. In every endeavor and activity in life, there is always a stipulated time for all kinds of choices to be actualized. Our choices determine our progress and speed through different stages of our lives. Timing is always crucial and is of the essence in regard to our choices.

Passion: Our passions directly or indirectly influence our choices. We cannot separate the choices we make from our passions, because our choices subtly control our actions which are fueled by our passions. Our choices demonstrate how passionate we are about certain things. The choices we make eventually align and actualize our actions to our passions.

Human beings are entities, of feelings and emotions, therefore, as such passions are common to all of us. We express our feelings and emotions via our choices to keep the flames of the things we are passionate about aflame.

Regrets are the dividend and by-product of bad and ill choices.

Regret: Our choices always create something in our lives and sometimes in the lives of others. They can create joy, happiness, contentment, satisfaction, peace, harmony, unity or pain, sorrow, stagnation, chaos, and regret.

Either way, every choice has the power to create something known and unknown. All of us have experienced one of the above at one stage or another in our lives, whether because of our choices or the choices of others.

This is why regret is common ground for all of us, and our past poor or bad choices fuel regret. Regrets are the dividends and by-products of poor, bad, or ill choices that we've made in the past.

CHOICES ARE FORERUNNERS

Mistakes and setbacks are some of the byproducts of poor, wrong, bad, and ill choices which eventually fuel regret in the future. The regret ground of choices is a place in life's journey where we have to bell the cat and drink the bitter waters of the bad, ill, or illicit choices we've made in our past.

Sometimes there are points in our lives where the only song that we will sing is the sad song of regret. We do this when we understand that we could have done something better than what we did or could have made a better choice than the one choice we made.

In such instances we are sometimes able to make amends for our past mistakes, but other times we cannot. Common areas where we might experience regrets include in our relationships, self-development, finances, and communication. For example:

- Not saying a simple thank you
- Living a lifestyle of entitlement
- Not telling loved ones how much we love them
- Not appreciating people who help us
- Being sarcastic to any form of help or kindness that we receive
- Not utilizing or investing our time in a productive manner

When we make poor, wrong, or bad choices, a wheel of regrets is automatically set-in motion. We have all made choices in the past and are perhaps still making choices that are creating regrets in our lives and in the lives of others.

Therefore, we must avert and halt the wheel of regret in our lives by not taking choices for granted and by taking responsibility for our lives and actions. We must also be continually thankful and not make choices flippantly no matter if they are trivial or serious.

Responsibility: This is common to all of us because we are each directly or indirectly accountable to someone or something. No one is an island; we all are dependent on each other. We all make choices that determine how we navigate our lives and that also determine the responses we receive from others.

Responsibility entails that life and society expect certain things from us and hold us accountable when necessary. It means that we are expected to take ownership of what life has placed in our laps.

Our choices concerning our duties influence our results in all areas of life whether we are great or small, strong or weak, wise or foolish. Our choices regarding our responsibilities reflects our commitment to a set goal or assignment. Throughout life we are constantly assigned one assignment or another and our choices while on assignment reflect our dedication.

Our choices that pertain to things we are responsible for in life determine how we will fair and thrive in our various assignments. Any attempt to ignore our responsibilities in any area of life or choose to either ignore an assignment or instruction can become a thorn in our flesh. How we choose to accept or deny our responsibilities in life can make us soar or fall.

> *Our choices can either strengthen or weaken our purpose in life.*

CHAPTER 6

CHOICES ARE INVITATIONS

IN LIFE, AN invitation is always synonymous with a request, call, enticement, bait. Hence, to invite someone means to request, call, entice, or bait them to something, for example, birthdays, house warmings, dates, thanksgiving parties, parent meetings in school, graduations, dedications, anniversaries, engagements, weddings, special times with family or friends, job interviews, business meetings, funerals, and more. These are the first things that normally come to mind when the word "invitation" is mentioned. However, when we only think of the word in that manner, we wind up limiting its full power. We minimize how crucially the word can make a difference in the choices we make, and we downplay how the word can be a trigger for making good or bad choices.

In all realms of life, we are repeatedly presented with a series of options to choose from. These options are presented to us as invitations. They are available to us in various situations that transpire throughout our lives. Invitations are presented to us as choices, and we have to choose either to accept or decline them. These invitations are issued both internally and externally and whatever invitation we accept becomes our choice.

CHOICES ARE FORERUNNERS

Most times though, people are only conscious of external invitations while they are unaware of internal invitations. Internal invitations are transactions of the mind which directly or indirectly propel our choices. Internal invitations can invite us to experience pleasure or pressure, joy or sadness, welfare or warfare, ease or torment, tranquility or turbulence, hate or love, and good or evil.

The truth about choices is that they are compilations of invitations and offers that are sent to each and every one of us internally and externally. Yet they only become authentic when we accept them.

Making choices is similar to accepting invitations and it is a place of making decisions.

In every sphere of life, choices are invitations issued consciously and subconsciously. All these invitations are either seen and unseen, tangible and intangible. They are issued on a daily basis and they become effective or ineffective, depending on the choices we make. For example, invitations to do good or evil, to love or hate are sent to us in our thoughts, emotions, and will, each and every day. They are issued by our mind, associations, or by events and transactions in our lives.

In spite of all these invitations that are issued, the reality and beauty of it all is that we still have the power and privilege to choose which of these invitations we will accept or ignore. This depends on our capacity to filter the invitations we receive in the Maze of Choices and how active our filtration system is.

It doesn't matter how many invitations are issued to us internally or externally. The only thing that matters is what we choose to accept. This is influenced by the strength of our filtration system, which is anchored by our mentalities, perspectives, perceptions, values, beliefs, morals, education, and priorities.

Choices Are Accessories

Our choices have the power to aggrandize or belittle people and situations.

Choices are like accessories that dress, complement, enhance, decorate, aggrandize, beautify, elevate, exalt, and strengthen us. Conversely, they can also undress, belittle, diminish, weaken, reduce, or downgrade us. It all depends on the choices we make. Our choices can enlist us or decommission us from opportunities and possibilities in life. They can also harmonize or disharmonize our lives. The power to choose is inherent in us as humans and God gave us the freedom to choose our paths in life.

Our choices can enlist us or decommission us from opportunities and possibilities in life.

Whatever we choose to do with our power of choice will reflect in our lives. Also, to some degree, it affects or blesses the lives of others. Not only do the choices we make individually and collectively affects or bless our lives and those close to us, our accumulated choices, also have the ability to affect and influence the lives of others known and unknown to us.

Choices can cause domino effects in the lives of others. Any wrong, bad, or poor choices made by an authority figure such as a politician, a doctor, teacher, pharmacist, head of a home, an executive, a chef, plumber, technician, or an engineer can have adverse effects on and in the lives of people who are directly or indirectly related them.

This is why choices are as critical to our lives as oxygen is to our bodies. Choices determine how we live, and they can affect the safety and the existence of others. Therefore, we must take the power to choose and our choices seriously in aspects of life.

Choices: The Place of Freedom

The ability to choose is a freedom we all share. However, true freedom is found only when we take responsibility for our choices.

We have the freedom to choose what we want and desire in every aspect, situation, and circumstance in life in spite of internal or external influences that might try to impede, propel, or corrupt our freedom to choose correctly.

This freedom to choose does not exempt us from taking responsibility for our choices because freedom without responsibility is destructive. That is why the place of choice is a place to exercise our will and take responsibility for the choices we made.

We can abuse our freedom to choose by not taking responsibility for our choices. This mindset can leave destructive results in its wake.

In every choice there is the underlying truth that is ever present. It is there regardless if the choice is good or bad choices. This underlying truth is freedom. It is the freedom to choose in almost all situations. Freedom is ever present in all the choices we make and is even present amid dangerous situations.

We must approach our freedom of choice with discipline because true freedom is found only when we are disciplined.

However, there are two sides to this freedom. It can be beneficial or harmful to us. It all depends on whether we make good or bad choices. In each case there is a learning process that takes place as we learn from the outcomes of our choices.

The choices that we make out of our free will always align with our desires. As a result, our choices reflect our true character. Yet how we exercise our freedom to choose is anchored by our internal and external strengths and priorities in all spheres of life.

The freedom to choose does not exempt us from taking responsibility for our choices.

Results, rewards, attainments, and punishments are products and by-products of our choices.

The Maze of Choice Is a Maze of Selection

Every choice empowers us with the freedom to select whatever we deem fit in a given situation. Making choices is the same thing as selecting something, and we always have the freedom to select from the multiple options presented at every situation.

The Maze of Choices can also be known as the maze of selection. In every aspect of life, we are bombarded on a daily basis with multiple options to choose from. Whatever we choose becomes our choice, and this will eventually decide, how we sail or anchor our life, boats in the race of life.

In the Maze of Choices, whatever we select or choose does not only affect or empower us, but other people who have to do with our power of selection. Whatever we select among the multitude of options life presents to us can also determine if the life, boats of other people under our influence will sail or sink.

In effect, our choices will determine the standard of our lives and of the lives of others. Subsequently, it can create stardom in our lives that attracts others. Whatever we select out of the options life present to us in the maze of selection has the power to empower us and others, especially when we choose correctly.

The Freedom to Choose Empowers Us

The freedom to make choices and selections empowers us. It empowers us and others to live our dreams and achieve our goals.

The ability to choose and make choices freely is an empowerment especially when the freedom is utilized positively. Our freedom to choose is our greatest asset in life because not everyone has this freedom.

Our freedom to choose is an asset that empowers us to create the life we desire. It is the tool we use to draw and map out our dreams and goals. We become the architects of our lives based on the choices we make.

Choices Are Investments

Choices are investments in our lives which eventually yield dividends at one point or another; however, the richness of the dividends depends on the choices that we've made. Our choices are investments for our future.

> ***Choices are investments that can produce satisfaction or dissatisfaction, pain or gain.***

While we might not always realize it, each of us are investors by nature because of our choices.

The irony of this is that both the rich and the poor are actively engaging in investing through their choices knowingly and unknowingly. It is our choices that dramatically differentiate us from others. Our choices produce rewards and consequences in our lives. They are investments that cover all the spheres of our lives such as, parenting, education, relationships, finances, and more, which are all affected by our choices. We are always consciously or subconsciously making one form of investment or another via our choices.

CHOICES ARE INVITATIONS

Choices, like investments, yield dividends in and for our future. For example, investing in oneself educationally and choosing to build a stable and strong financial future by delaying one's gratification is an investment triggered by the power of choice.

Choosing to invest time to nurture and groom our children and relationships is an investment. These kinds of investments are beneficial to everyone. Poor choices like choosing the route of not investing in oneself or others are also investments that will definitely yield zero interest.

The choices we make today are the initiators of every transaction that will transpire in our tomorrows. We must remember that we can only invest in the moment and the future. We cannot invest in our past or turn back time; neither can we retrieve yesterday, so we have to always choose wisely.

Also, it is important to think before making any choice because certain choices made might be hard to undo once the choice wheel has been set in motion. Likewise, we must try as much as possible to make choices that will be profitable to us and others in order to avoid regrets.

> *We create some circumstances in our lives by the choices we make, and we can also change certain circumstances in our lives by the choices we make.*

CHAPTER 7

BY CHOICE

EVERY ACTIVITY AND transaction in the streets of life that is orchestrated by human beings is triggered by the choices we make and act upon. Whatever we choose to do or refuse to do in any given area of life is by choice. We live our lives by the choices we make in different areas of life, and whatever our choices produce in our lives becomes our rewards or punishments.

In every circumstance of life, it is normal and expected of us to make a choice. Whatever we choose to do or refuse to do in life is by choice. This includes every action and step that we take in life. Our survival, success, or failure in any area of life depends on the choices we make, individually and collectively. Wherever we might be at this moment in our lives, it is being orchestrated by the choices we've made individually and by the choices of others. We can control certain events in our lives by the choices we make. This is because in most issues of life, we have the power of choice at our disposal.

Below are some examples of activities, attitudes, and behaviors that we engage in and that pertain to our choices.

CHOICES ARE FORERUNNERS

Being Abusive—To be abusive is a choice. To be disrespectful and treat others with cruelty is by choice irrespective of the reasons we try to give to justify such behaviors.

Abusive choices include verbal abuse, physical abuse, access abuse, emotional abuse, relationship abuse, trust abuse, mental abuse, and misuse and abuse of one's position or privileges. Using our office or position as an opportunity to oppress others under our domain is wrong and in error. Abusive choices are error that must be corrected.

Every official position in the society was meant for the edification of people and not for their oppression.

Whatever form of abusive behavior we choose to engage in during our personal or collective dealings with others, always remember there is always a better choice we can make.

Abusive choices cause pain in others and they place limitations on the abuser.

Abusive choices cause the abuse victims pain and harm. All abusive choices always birth the negative in the lives of the recipients and also in the lives of the one making the choice to be abusive.

However, it is imperative to know that there are some cases where some abusive choices made in the past can be rectified, but there are other cases where the damage is irreversible or irrevocable. Either way, all abusive choices hamper and tamper with the welfare of others by dampening their joy and peace.

Anger—Anger is the advance phase of offence; it is the metamorphosed form of offence. As human beings, the chances are always there that someone will step on our toes. How we handle the offence will determine if the offence will transform into anger. We all have nurtured offence into anger at one area of our lives or another.

Even when we are angry, we still have the power to choose if we will allow the sun to set on our anger or not. Whenever we make the choice to allow the sun to set on our anger, we automatically transfer our power to choose to our anger and to the person or people who offended us. We must choose to control ourselves and refrain from anger, even when there are legitimate reasons to be angry. Any time we lose control of our emotions by yielding to the force of anger, we run the risk of making irrational decisions.

Once we yield to the force of anger, we automatically relinquish our power of choice to the situation or person that has offended us. At the end, we are no longer in control of the situation, which can lead, to lose of self-control. When we are void of the power to choose, we are void of the power to influence, control, or determine the situation and outcome.

Excuses—Excuse is a double-sided word that carries the characteristic of truth and falsehood, depending on its usage. It can be the highway whereby we dodge our responsibility or a medium to express a truthful circumstantial mishap or shortcoming.

Most of the time, excuses are killers of potential and opportunities. It is the pathway of laziness when we use excuses as a tool of falsehood. Making excuses and using excuses as avenues to dodge our responsibilities is by choice. It is a choice most of us are unconsciously making without realizing the damage or hurt we are invoking on ourselves. It is a choice made to, knowingly and unknowingly, look for a reason or reasons to dodge our responsibilities.

Making excuses to cover our shortcoming and negligence is a platform to become irresponsible; irresponsibility that is fueled by the reasons that we use to try to support and make our excuses authentic. Most times, we make excuses to dodge our responsibilities, which in turn engenders failures and setbacks in our lives. Sometimes in the Maze of Choices, we even use excuses as weapons against ourselves.

Some of us are not even aware of the fact that any time we find a suitable reason or reasons not to take ownership of our responsibilities, directly or indirectly, we have signed up to fail in that given area. Therefore, to avoid the mishap of excuses, it is crucial to consciously and intentionally make the choice not to use excuses as an avenue to dodge our responsibilities, even when there are legitimate reasons to support it.

Going the Extra Mile—All activities and endeavors are being fulfilled or executed by the choices we make in different areas of life. Our choices determine how successful we will be. In addition, our willingness to be successful in any area of life is a trigger, which propels us to invest more of our time, resources, and knowledge into achieving success

We can only reach the bar of success that we set for ourselves by choice. Doing things beyond the conventional entails going the extra mile in order to achieve our goals.

Choosing to go the extra mile will always cause us to stretch beyond our comfort zone. It is a choice that will take us to the place where we have to endure inconvenience in order to attain certain goals or fulfill our dreams. Choosing to go the extra mile in any endeavor will certainly create some hiccups. However, the end results outweigh the discomfort we might experience along the way. In the success equation, going the extra mile to attain our goals is a constant and dominant factor that is common in all success stories.

> *Knowledge is gained through learning. Anyone who refuses to learn will reap and eat the fruits of ignorance.*

Learning—Learning is by choice. We choose to have an open mind and to be receptive to new ideas and possibilities; to practice and put into action what has been taught. Choosing to learn makes us grow and not become static.

Learning takes place when we individually, or as a group, choose to learn new things. This choice is completed when we apply what we have learned to solve issues and enhance our standard of living, in order to initiate change and growth in the area of life where the insight has been gained.

By choice, we as humans have the possibility to learn and broaden our knowledge. Therefore, the learning choice teaches us that we are not omniscient but nescient in certain areas of life, and we have to choose to humble ourselves and open up to learn from others who have in-depth knowledge in areas where we lack knowledge.

The desire not to be ignorant in any particular area is a desire for knowledge, and knowledge is the propeller that propels us to learn. By choice we learn new skills, acquire new information, and broaden our knowledge in any subject.

In any area of life in which we choose to learn, we're automatically improving and upgrading ourselves.

Learning is also a continuous process that we must activate on a daily basis in our lives because by choice we learn and by choice we also relearn, unlearn, and choose not to learn.

> **Even though learning is part of life, we must still make a conscious choice to learn.**

The day we choose to stop learning is the day we begin to regress in life. We must all choose and be committed to learn; being on the continuous learning mode is a choice we all must make in all areas of life in order for us to be useful to ourselves and others. Every day, we by choice are consciously or subconsciously engaging in one form of learning and another.

Boldness and Daring—There is no attainment or success in any area of life without boldness and daring to explore the unknown. Neither is there any victory without boldness or by daring to achieve that which seems impossible. To achieve anything in life, we must choose to be bold and daring in order to make our goals a reality. We must intentionally choose to confront the impossible and the unknown.

Boldness and daring are also two-sided words, which can have positive and negative effects. In this book, we consider boldness and daring from a positive perspective. Boldness and daring empower us to explore the hidden potential in us and around us. They make us to realize that all positive heights are attainable, and we can overcome any obstacles in our way to achieve our goals and dreams.

We must be bold enough to dream. That level of boldness is the hallmark of successful people. We must dare to explore new ground. We must choose to take risks, for risks are behind every new innovation in our world today. Being bold and daring means that we don't pay attention to mockers; neither to those who tell us we can't achieve our goals. Instead, we keep our eyes firmly set on our goals. In the end, it also takes boldness to see prospects in the midst of chaos and treasures where others see impossibilities.

Cover Ups—It is by choice to make wrong look good, and we choose to cover up bad things in order to look good in the short term. In so doing, we choose to not see beyond the enticing bait of the moment, and we succumb to our desire for immediate gratification and our desire to satisfy a lust or craving.

We use excuses and cover ups as escape route to cover up inadequacy and weakness; however, it is difficult to cover up truth in the long term because truth always has a way of prevailing at the end.

Covering something up only gives us respite for a season. Ultimately choosing to cover something up costs more in the long run as its ramifications will eventually rear their ugly heads.

Extreme Criticism—We choose to be critical. Most of the time a critical attitude only results in negative feeling because uncontrolled criticism sucks out the oxygen in any environment, turning it toxic.

Any criticism in the Maze of Choices that is positively motivated empowers us and others to aim higher in order to perform better, to attain perfection in any desired endeavor. However, extreme criticism that is negatively motivated is a means to self-condemnation of ourselves and others. Extreme criticism is a weapon, which we use knowingly or unknowingly to hurt ourselves and others. It can also be seen from different perspectives by people; for example:

- As a source of empowerment
- A pointer for perfection
- An avenue to ridicule or belittle others
- A point of gossip

It is crucial to know that every criticism is target-specific and goal-oriented because behind every criticism, there is a motive and intention, which act as triggers for the criticism. Knowing the motive and intentions behind any criticism helps us to identify the aim of the critics.

The choice to be extremely critical all the time and not see the good in others or things is a dangerous path in the Maze of Choices. It limits us and others and sometimes drains the self-confidence and self-esteem of others. When we choose to be critical all the time, we have unknowingly placed an embargo on ourselves and others.

To be extremely critical is by choice; it is a choice made to find fault in others and sometimes in ourselves individually. It is ok to criticize oneself but not to the degree of becoming our own enemies. In fact, it is quite dangerous to be our own critic. Being our own personal critic can become an avenue to cripple our destinies when it is taken to the extreme.

Most people subconsciously choose to be their own worst enemy because of how critical they have become in judging themselves as people not good enough or people who don't deserve the good things or privileges of life. The choice to be critical all the time can rob us of the ability to fully tap into our potential because constant self-criticism drains our motivation. The choice made to be critical in one area of life can slip and affect other areas of life, because criticism is like a parasitic root that digs into other areas in our lives.

Discouragement—In life there are many situations and happenings that we will encounter that will discourage us. In spite of the challenges that might be confronting us in any area of life, we still have a choice to make on how we will respond to them. Sometimes in life, when it seems all hope is lost, it is easy to choose to be discouraged; however, we still have a choice to make to either look for the silver lining in the situation or become discouraged.

At one point or another in the Maze of Choices, discouragement can cause us to get caught up in a web of entanglement. This happens when we choose to focus more on the dilapidating situations when combating the curveballs of life.

Discouragement becomes a choice when we directly or indirectly choose to throw in the towel amid life's turbulence and challenges. Whenever we choose to take the route of discouragement in the Maze of Choices, it tempers and redirects our focus. This eventually fuels the force of discouragement in our lives even more.

Victory is inevitable when we choose to not be discouraged in the midst of life's curve balls.

Encouragement—To be encouraged is by choice. We choose to be encouraged each and every day of our lives, even at times when life is not a bed of roses. At every junction in life, the first encourager you will need is **YOU.**

There are times in life when we have to encourage ourselves, especially when nobody believes in us. Thus, we have to choose to be our own encouragers, supporters, and fans. As humans, there will come a time in life when we have to individually carry our crosses, and our abilities to carry our crosses on our own is proportional to the choices we have made individually—to be encouraged or discouraged.

In our society today, "sponsorship" is a word that has been interwoven with many transactions in different spectrums of life. In our lives there are areas where, at one point or another, we must choose to be our own sponsors, and one of those areas is the area of self-encouragement, where we are the major sponsor of our encouragement. To be self-encouraged is a choice and once that choice is made, the possibility to be easily conquered or be a victim of circumstances is minimized.

Of course, we all need encouragement from other people at one point and another in our lives, but still, it is our individual responsibility to keep encouraging ourselves amid life's challenges. If peradventure there are people in our lives that are our supporters and encouragers, it is ok to embrace them. But if not, we have to make the choice to be encouraged in spite of the prevailing situations or happenings.

The Fighter Spirit—In life's journey, there are challenging times and seasons, and it takes the fighter spirit to keep us from being swallowed up by the challenges of life. Each and every one of us has the fighter spirit inside us, and it is often active in some areas of our lives more than others.

While, to some of us, the fighter spirit is all-around active in all areas of life and, unfortunately, some people have put the fighter spirit in them to sleep by the choices they make amid challenges. This is an error, so it is crucial to be aware that it is by choice we awaken the fighter spirit within us. It is a choice we have to make daily in different aspects of our lives. It is a choice we must make never to give up amid the battles of life lest we become a casualty in life's battle fields.

The fighter spirit does not engage in physical fights or power tussles, but mental fights in our minds.

The fighter spirit is the spirit of determination engaged by choice. It means that we do not accept failure as the end or the ultimate finale of our lives. It is a spirit that keeps fighting and will not throw in the towel in spite of past or current failures. It is the choice made to keep standing in spite of the numerous falls we might have experienced in life. It takes a fighter spirit to avoid self-pity as we choose to stand up no matter the adversity or challenges. The fighter spirit is the fuel that boosts the mentality of not giving in, giving way, or giving up amid challenges.

The fighter spirit uses others mocking us as fuel to gain momentum/ strength even when all odds are against us. The fighter spirit is the conqueror's spirit that aims at victory. The fighter spirit stands alone when others leave and it is a prevailing, inherent force in each of us that will not surrender to any worrisome circumstance or adversity, and it can only be activated by choice.

Forgiveness—Forgiveness is a key to our freedom and well-being in all areas of life. We choose to forgive those who offend or do us wrong. To forgive those who treat us unkindly is a choice, and it carries a great reward with it that is beneficial to us.

The choice made to forgive is a gift to the forgiver and the offender. It is a gift we alone can give to ourselves in any situation. The force of forgiveness is activated by choice, which automatically gives us justice when we choose to forgive, whether the offender apologizes or not.

Forgiveness is a key in our hands which we use to control our own emotions, and it frees us from being controlled by the emotions of others. Forgiveness brings us to a place of empowerment and freedom. It gives us the freedom to be ourselves and live our lives on our own terms.

In the Maze of Choices, forgiveness is not foolishness or a sign of weakness. Rather it is a healing balm we use to treat the hurts inflicted on us by the wrong doings of others. Forgiveness and tolerance are not always about the offender. Rather they are about us choosing to live our lives without carrying others' baggage. It is all about us choosing to enjoy life and not to be embittered by the offences from others.

That being said, forgiveness does not mean fraternizing with the offender; it means releasing the offender from the prison of our hearts so that we do not incapacitate our focus and performance.

Gratitude and Appreciation—We must choose to be grateful and appreciative. When we do, it opens us up to new opportunities. Gratitude and appreciation are springboards for us to access greater things in life. They help us engender favor, kindness, and goodwill from others. We must also choose to recognize and appreciates the good gestures of others and to appreciate the little things in life and never take anything for granted.

Being grateful and appreciative are seeds we sow in different areas of life. They eventually produce fruits in our lives. Thankfulness and appreciation are the keys for getting more out of life. Gratitude and appreciation are triggers for multiplication and to experiencing life more abundantly.

Joyfulness—We choose to be joyful. It is a choice that solemnly depends on us individually to make and not on others. We must consciously and intentionally choose to be joyful because nothing can make us joyful, not people or situations, unless we choose to be.

> *Joy is contagious! It has the power to attract people to us.*

Joy is not a gift but a matter of choice. In life, we are the ones who have to choose whether to be joyful or not. To be joyful is by choice, a choice that might be difficult to make amid prevailing challenges of life. It's a choice we must make irrespective of the challenges. In the Maze of Choices amid challenges, having hope is a catalyst for joy, and feeding our hope in any situation will make it much easier for us to be joyful.

Hope and joy are connected because once there is hope in any situation, there is always a reason not to give up or be sad. Hope is the silver lining in any situation. Wherever there is hope, joy is always present because it is hope that keeps joy alive. In every unpleasant situation, we have a choice to make, whether we will be joyful or not. Whatever choice we make is made internally, which will eventually bust out externally. Our joy is triggered internally and seen externally.

Joy is contagious! It has the power to attract people to us. It has the ability to rub off on others positively. It is by choice we create joy-filled atmospheres in our lives. To be joyful is a wise choice that empowers us to attain the impossible in the midst of life's curveballs.

We always have access to knowledge, but we must choose to acquire it.

Knowledge—If we don't acquire knowledge, we will easily go astray in life. That is why knowledge is vital and nonnegotiable to our lives and to our choices. We must choose to be willing and open to learning. It is through learning and understanding that knowledge is acquired. Every insight we gain gives us a greater advantage over others.

If we don't acquire knowledge we will easily go astray in life. That is why knowledge is vital and nonnegotiable to our life and to our choices.

Positive knowledge that we gain has the power to influence, enlighten, empower, and equip us to succeed in the areas where we make choices go for more knowledge. Any knowledge gained broadens and increases our depth of insight, which eventually enhances our lives and helps us to see things from different perspectives.

Knowledge enables us to make judgments in light of the information at our disposal, especially when the knowledge gained is true and authentic.

The beauty of nurturing others brings nourishment to those being nurtured and the person nurturing, in

> *terms of physical, mental, social, emotional, moral, educational, and spiritual nourishment.*

Nurture—We choose to nurture and nourish ourselves and others. It is a choice we make to care for ourselves and extend a caring, supportive, and helping hand to others in need. To nurture and nourish others is a process of incubating them in times of need, especially when life's curveballs are being served in different areas of their lives.

This also means that we make a choice not to give up on ourselves or others, especially when people have written us off or given up on us. It means that we do not let the flame of greatness in us and others go out. Nurturing and nourishment fan the fires of possibility in our lives and in the lives of others. This gives people hope amid hopeless situations.

For different people, this choice is made consciously and subconsciously. Those who nurture others continually form a habit by which the choice becomes natural to them. These individuals are warm and caring. They choose to make a difference in the lives of others by nurturing others to discover and cultivate the gifts embedded in them that might be known or unknown to them.

Nurturing people are selfless, and their actions add value to their lives and to the lives of others. They show kindness and not wickedness. They extend a hand of fellowship and redirect those who have gone off course back to the right path. They speak words of wisdom and build people up to greatness.

> *Submission or obedience to instruction, laws, and rules engender peace, tranquility, and order in all spheres of life.*

Obedience—The act, practice, or quality to be obedient or submissive to a rule or authority is by choice. Obedience to authority, laws, or rules is mandatory, but the reality is it is by choice we abide by the law. Even if a law or rule is mandatory, it does not mean people will abide or play by the book. Although there are rules and laws enacted to be obeyed in all spheres of life by those under a jurisdiction, most times people choose not to obey these laws or rules, which can result in consequences that might be detrimental to them.

However, obedience fosters peace and tranquility. We must be obedient to rules and laws in order to avoid potholes and heartache. Obedience to rules keeps us going in the right direction in life. Thus, obedience is a core path through life that can benefit us greatly when we stick to it.

Obedience fosters peace and tranquility.

Obedience means that we comply to instruction. Obedience can be delayed or prompt. In any area of life, we are prompted to obey an instruction, rule, or law, it is triggered by choice; a choice that will birth the predictable consequences, which is/are outlined in the law or instruction.

Offensiveness—We choose to be offended with ourselves and others, and this will rob us of positive emotions and energy. Even in situations where we have been unduly wronged, we still have the power to decide how we will respond or react. Of course, it is ok to be angry or be offended if we have been done wrong but not to the extent that we lose our ability to think rationally. Letting anger take over can actually be detrimental to our lives.

To live in offence is by choice, and this choice has the power to place a limitation and embargo in different areas of life, such as our dealings and relationships with others. Offence, when it is not dealt with, can lead to bitterness, and bitterness can become a root for desiring the downfall of the offender. Offence is the sponsor of bitterness, anger and rancor, bad will, and hatred.

The effects of offence are seen in two dimensions—in the lives of the offender and the offended. The effect is harmful, and it has the power to incapacitate both parties.

Choosing the path not to be offended is not an easy choice to make neither is it pain-free; however, it is more profitable to live a life void of offence. This is possible by continuously exercising our consciences to make intentional choices amid offensive behavior and happenings. It is a difficult choice to make amid hurting or offensive situations, but it is a choice that needs to be made daily because there are always people that will be constant triggers of offence in our lives.

In as much as there are people who will offend us, the power to respond lies in our hands. Hence, people might be triggers of offence, but we have the power of choice—the power to dodge their bullets of offence—which is only possible by choice.

Selfishness—To be deficient in having consideration for others' well-being and welfare is by choice. No one was born to be selfish. Being selfish is by choice. We choose to be more concerned about ourselves than others, even if this is to their detriment. Selfishness is embodied in a "me first" mentality where a person will go to any length to achieve their own selfish desires, irrespective of the chaos it might create in the lives of others.

In the Maze of Choices, most people choose to act selfishly. That is why selfishness is a major sponsor of the backstabbing that is actively transpiring in different spectrums in our world today. Selfishness is a driving force in most transactions in the streets of life and is the sponsor of the downfall of many where people make choices to satisfy their selfish interests to the detriment of others. Selfishness is the opposite of selflessness. Selfishness is a choice people make consciously and it can become automatic if not dealt with on time.

Self-Control—Having self-control in different areas of life is by choice. The choice made to put oneself under self-restriction pertains to issues and happenings, especially in turbulent times. Self-control is our ability to control ourselves, especially our emotions and desires, in difficult situation. We must choose to maintain self-control in unpleasant situations because there are always situations and people who will be in our lives who will test the strength of our self-control in different areas of life.

Self-control helps us avoid irrational judgment because self-control is like a good seed that always bears good fruits. In all spheres of life, self-control is the choice seed that puts us automatically in charge of situations. It enables us to weigh and see things from different perspectives and angles before taking action in any situation. Having self-control empowers us to have an in-depth insight into any situation we choose to engage the force of self-control in.

Whenever we make the choice to engage the force of self-control in any situation that might be uncomfortable or painful, the outcome is always more palatable. Amid all the troubling situations in life, the choice to remain calm and have self-control, in spite of odd emotions that the situations might be brewing, puts us automatically in charge.

Self-control is a weapon that puts us in charge of our emotions, responses, and, to some extent, others and situations. Engaging in self-control ensures that our emotions do not control our actions. Self-control builds inner strength and peace that enable us to stand firm amid turbulent times. Self-control puts us in charge of situations instead of situations taking charge of us or being in charge of us.

Self-Limitation—Sometimes in life we subconsciously place limitations on ourselves by the choices we make without being aware of it. These choices range from using belittling words consciously and subconsciously on ourselves to the actions we engage in and how we present ourselves before others.

All these can place hindrances on us that can become sources of limitation in our lives. Once we personally place any limitation on ourselves via the choices we make, it automatically creates an avenue for others to use and abuse us for their selfish interests.

There are certain phrases we as human beings use to place limitations on ourselves, and such phrases act as signals for others to take advantage of us if we are not careful. Such phrases include:

- "I can't do it."
- "It's too difficult."
- "It's not possible."
- "Who will help me?"
- "I'm not good enough."
- "No one is interested in me."
- "I'm from a poor background."
- "It's not meant for people like me."
- "I don't have the ability or capacity to do it."

Whenever we use such phrases, we place limitations on ourselves, even when we have not tried or attempted to tackle those things that seem impossible to us. By using such phrases to address ourselves, we've automatically deleted ourselves from viable opportunities.

Whenever we make choices that place limitations on us, we unknowingly program ourselves to be on continuous delete mode. We also use our past experiences, especially the bad experiences, as stumbling blocks that influence our choices. Simply put, our past choices can limit us today.

Our self-limiting choices place restrictions on us, which can also interfere with other areas of our lives where the choices were not initially made. This diminishes the possibility for us to grow, increase, or soar. Self-limiting choices are terrible self-sentences people place on themselves.

Taking Responsibility—In life we are expected to take responsibility for various things and sometimes it is even mandatory to do so. The reality is we choose to take responsibility in our lives.

We still have a choice to make in order to meet standards and fulfill our duties. Taking responsibility in any sphere of life always demands and costs us something in terms of energy, time, resources. Still, the rewards are well worth the cost.

As long as we are alive, we all are accountable to certain laws and rules that govern different aspects of our lives. We are expected to diligently execute our responsibilities by complying with the rules that govern different areas of life, whether we want to or not. The choice to take responsibility entails taking ownership of an assignment assigned to us and ensuring that the assignment is executed to the expected standard. Any aspect of life where we choose to take responsibility for our actions, dealings, and duties automatically positions us for recognition.

Whenever we choose to take responsibility in any sphere of life, we are put on a pedestal to learn and acquire the necessary knowledge to grow and increase our capacity. Taking responsibility helps us to set a standard for ourselves, to have boundaries, also to know what is acceptable and expected of us. In the end, taking responsibility acts as a compass that helps direct our path in life.

Respect—Respect is the willingness to value and esteem ourselves, and others in spite of our differences, races, or positions. It means that we choose to respect others for who they are. Respect is a choice because every one of us has the freedom to choose what to admire, esteem, and recognize in others. It is the act of acknowledging others based on the attributes we choose to see in them.

To be respectful is a learned behavior and it can become automatic through continuous practice. The choice to respect others and their boundaries is consciously and intentionally triggered. Respect is like a sound that goes or vibrates out and reverberates back to the sender.

It is like a two-sided coin that has equal value; hence, the vibration we send out in the form of respect to others has a way of catching up with us. Being respectful means we send out sound words of kindness, honor, appreciation, adoration, and approval to the world.

Whenever, we make the choice to operate and deal with others respectfully, it affects and controls the atmosphere by making it cordial, welcoming, and warm for all. Likewise, when we choose to operate and deal with others with disrespect, it affects the environment by making it toxic and hostile.

To be respectful or disrespectful both have the power to determine and control the atmospheric condition of any place or environment. It is crucial to know and always remember that any hostile atmosphere is mostly triggered by the choice made by a person or group of people to disrespect others. To respect others irrespective of their positions or statuses is by choice. It is a choice that creates an ambience of civility for all. Therefore, by choice, we all are in charge to control the atmospheric conditions in our environments.

Time Investment—Time is an essential component used to measure our lifespans on earth. It encompasses the duration of various transactions, events, and seasons in our lives. Time is an essential treasure that is irreplaceable, not transferable, and cannot be pre-ordered in advance. Each of us chooses what we do with our own time. We all choose to invest or waste our time consciously, subconsciously, and sometimes intentionally.

Time is an essential treasure in life. It is irreplaceable and non-transferable, and it cannot be pre-ordered in advance.

How we choose to spend our time will determine our results and outcomes in life. All of the activities that we engage in are time oriented and time-consuming. Time is a gift to humanity and all of us, are given equal allocation. However, how we choose to invest our time differs depending on the choices we make individually or collectively as a group.

Whether we are spending, investing, or wasting our time is a choice each and every one of us makes, knowingly and unknowingly, every second, minute, and hour of every day. Time is one of the crucial treasures in life that cannot be retrieved, recovered, withheld, or kept still once it starts ticking.

When we choose individually or collectively as a group to waste our time, it is a choice that will profit us nothing and that will only create regrets. Likewise, if we choose to engage our time wisely by investing our time intentionally in more productive and profitable endeavors, the outcome is always profitable and beneficial to all.

How we choose to spend our time, either by investing, or wasting it, will influence and determine our futures. Our profitability in different aspects is anchored on the value we place on our time. Time is a vital gift to us as human beings.

Whether we are aware of it or not, we are either actively engaging our time wisely or unwisely. Therefore, we have to consciously and intentionally make choices correctly on how we invest our time on ourselves and others. Our time can become an investment in our lives and in the lives of others when we use it wisely.

Yielding and Resisting—Every day, from the rising of the sun to the going down of the sun, all activities that occur in the streets of life are guided by the force of yielding and resisting. We choose to yield to something or resist something. Both have is advantages and disadvantages; it all depends on what the situation entails.

All activities and transactions in the streets of life are triggered by choice, and all choices made in different spheres of life are controlled by the forces of yielding or resisting. The choice made at different situations of life always reflects what we are yielding to or resisting in our lives. Below are some examples of things that we yield to or resist:

- To love is yielding to the force of love and resisting the force of hate.

- To be joyful is yielding to the force of joy and resisting the forces of sadness or depression.

- To be obedient is yielding to the force of obedience and resisting the force of disobedience.

- To be kind is yielding to the force of kindness and resisting the force of selfishness.

- To be angry is yielding to the force of anger instead of yielding to self-control.

- To be respectful is yielding to the force of respect and resisting the force of disrespect.

- To be encouraged amid unpleasant or challenging situations is yielding to the force of encouragement and resisting the force of discouragement.

- To be grateful is yielding to the forces of appreciation and gratitude and resisting the force of ingratitude.

Whatever we do as we make choices in different areas of life; we are either yielding to or resisting choices. Finally, whatever choices we make in different situations or happenings in our lives, we need to realize that they can be premeditated or impromptu. Both of them have their own benefits and disadvantages.

Premediated and Impromptu Choices

In all aspects of life, we are daily confronted with issues and choices. Our choices can have a profoundly positive or negative outcome in our lives, and they can be made causally in an impromptu manner or premeditatedly. Therefore, choices can be calculated or impulsive, and both have the power to produce an outcome in our lives, which will eventually influence and control our futures.

CHOICES ARE FORERUNNERS

Premeditated Choices—Premeditated choices are calculated and organized choices. These are made when we deeply engage our minds and the power of reasoning to analyze the options available before making any choices.

To meditate or think before making any choice enable us to have a preview of the possible outcomes related to the choice. It is a dimension of choice-making where we cannot fully envision the outcome of our choices but have a glimpse of the possible outcomes. Premeditated choices are made in anticipation of producing a desired outcome or result.

In making premediated choices, different factors influence us. These factors vary from situation to situation and person to person. Premediated or calculative choices can be triggered by the following:

- Association
- Awareness
- Belief
- Desires
- Dreams
- Dissatisfaction
- Emotions
- Goals
- Health Conditions
- Knowledge
- Maturity
- Mindset
- Perspective
- Purpose

- Responsibility
- Status

All these factors have a way of influencing and engendering premediated choices, which can have a positive or negative outcome.

Impromptu Choices—These are choices usually made at the spur of the moment. They might not engage the future at all and as such they can create wanted or unwanted outcomes. These choices only focus on immediate gratification. There are times where impromptu choices result in a positive outcome, but there are also situations where it might result in negative outcomes.

The outcome of an impromptu choice depends on the circumstances and what the choice entails. Impromptu choices can result in regrets or become a ladder or bridge over raging waters. They can be productive or destructive in nature; it all depends on the force propelling the choices.

Both premediated and impromptu choices have an element of risk involved in them because they are each adventurous choices by nature. As such, we cannot fully predict the outcome of the premediated and impromptu choices.

> **The Maze of Choices is the place of programing one's life and destiny.**

CHAPTER 8

THE MAZE OF CHOICES

CHOICES ARE MADE by people and we, as human beings, have the freedom to choose our paths in the Maze of Choices. In every area of life, even in tough and difficult situations, we most times have the opportunity to choose the path we want to embark on.

Likewise, in the Maze of Choices, there are different categories of people present. It is quite interesting to know that at one point or phase in life, we might have fallen into one or more of these groups of people, depending on the choices we might have made based on our perceptions, principles, situations, and knowledge. Below are some examples:

- The Defensive Group
- The Emotional Group
- The Followers Group
- The Ignorant Group
- The Learned Group
- The Manipulating Group

CHOICES ARE FORERUNNERS

- The Obligatory Group
- The Risky Group
- The Selfish Group
- The Shadow Group
- The survival Group
- The Thoughtful Group

The Defensive Group—In the Maze of Choices, there are two sets of people on the defensive group:

- The Selfishly defensive
- The Selflessly defensive

The selfishly *defensive group:* This group of people make choices to satisfy their selfish interests, and they are always on the defensive to protect their personal gain. Most of the choices they make are targeted to defending all they do, even when they are doing the wrong thing. They will stand up to give reasons why they have chosen the route they have taken and will go to any length to pass blames on others in order to get whatever they want. They always have a cogent reason to back up their ill choices, even to the detriment of others.

The selflessly *defensive group*: This group of people make their choices solely to protect and guide others and themselves. Their main goal in the Maze of Choices is to attain a specific goal for the benefit of all. They are defensive for good reasons; they are on the defensive on behalf of themselves and others. The choices they make in the Maze of Choices are for the best interest, and vindication, of everyone.

The Emotional Group—This group of people allow their emotions to control their choices. Although we all, at one point or another, have been controlled by our emotions in making choices, the emotional group of people are constantly making choices based on their emotional state, because they allow their emotions to control their choices.

There are two groups of people in the Emotional Group—the *Extreme* and the *Moderate* groups. The extreme ones are like the weather, they are constantly changing, and fluctuating based on their emotional states; they are irrational and unpredictable. They act childishly and throw tantrums, especially when their emotional feathers are being ruffled in unpleasant ways.

The moderate group is able to put a lid over their emotions when making choices. They are rational and do not allow their emotions to impede or influence the choices they make. They remain in charge of their emotions instead of allowing their emotions to control the choices they make. They might fall sometimes, but they are quick in regaining control of their emotions in order to avert being ensnared by their emotions in the Maze of Choices.

The Followers Group—This group of people is engaged in making choices based on the instructions of others: their affiliation to an organization, a group or association, or to a person influences their choices directly or indirectly; hence, they do not have the mind or capacity to make their own choices. They make choices based on the doctrine, principles, ideology, and beliefs of others. Though this group of people might not have taken any oath, but they've consciously made the choice to become a follower of a person, a group, or an ideology. Some of them in this group have been brainwashed, while others are quite knowledgeable about the pros and cons but still choose to become followers.

Even when they are fully aware that the choices they are making might result in grievous consequences, which might be detrimental to them, members of the followers, group still choose to follow the path that aligns them with their affiliate group or association.

The Ignorant Group—This is a group of people who make choices on issues they do not have any real knowledge of or a full scoop on. They make choices based on assumptions and other people's opinion or choices. They actually make choices without knowing the full implication of the choices they are making. They are the bandwagon group who follow the crowd without actually knowing the destination or the direction of the journey.

They are the group who is being carried about by the current that flows through their lives. Their choices are being determined by the atmospheric condition around them. This atmospheric condition can be in the form of human or circumstantial influences. This group lacks the knowledge or has no awareness concerning the situation. They make choice without knowing the implication or the gravity of their choices, and the end result can sometimes be devastating.

The Learned Group—The Learned group is comprised of those who have insight about things. This group takes time to study and learn things about the prevailing situations that involve their choices. In some cases, they have done their own personal research concerning a particular area and have gained insight that eventually enlightens them in order to make the right choice in that particular area of their lives.

This group might not necessarily be educated in terms of having an educational degree, but they have taken it as a responsibility to enlighten themselves in any given situation before making a choice. They are the group that has learned from the events and transactions of their lives to make sound and gainful choices.

The Manipulating Group—In the Maze of Choices, the manipulating group is comprised of people who make choices primarily to exploit others. They are conniving and convincing in their dealings with others. This group of people specializes in manipulating other people into make choices that will be profitable to them, irrespective of the discomfort or harm it might cause their victims. They are the commanders in chief in manipulating others to get their desires or goals met at any given endeavor.

The members of this group are in the business of using others' mental or emotional weaknesses for their own benefit. They take advantage of the weakest link in the streets of life. The manipulators in the

Maze of Choices make choices based on their own interests and they will go to any length to get what they want, regardless of who their choices might hurt or harm.

The Obligation Group—There are two different types of people in the Obligation group:

- The Oath group
- The Responsibility group

In the Maze of Choices, each group makes choices for different reasons: one group, out of covenant; and the other group, out of responsibility. There is a tiny line of difference between both.

The Oath group: This group of people makes choices based on obligation. These obligations might be initiated by their alliance to certain groups, organizations, or fraternities to which they are bound to comply and make choices that will benefit the constitution of their organization or fraternity. Even when it is to their own detriment, this group will still choose to stay in the path of obligation. This group is different from the follower group, because they might know the right thing but, because of their obligation to certain people in their lives, they will choose to make the choice that will confirm their eternal support. This may be because of the oath or pledge they have made to a person, group, or organization.

This group is bound by an oath to comply with the constitution of the organization they belong to. Their freedom to choose, which is a free gift to humanity, is perverted because of the oath they taken. This group of people will never stand for the truth when it does not align with the constitution of their organization or fraternity. They will rather choose to pervert the truth in order not to break the oath or upset the status quo of their group or their organization.

The Responsibility group: This group of people makes choices based on their responsibility to do the right thing, the thing that will be favorable for humanity. They still have the power to choose and the freedom to choose what interests them. Because they are always conscious of the fact that there are consequences for not taking responsibility, all the choices they make are anchored on responsibility, even when it might be detrimental to them.

The Risky Group—This group of people gets pleasure from taking risks, even when they are quite dangerous or might be harmful to them. They enjoy and make it a lifestyle to engage in risky endeavors. They see life as an adventure and making risky choice makes life worth living for them. They are daily seeking out risky choices in any endeavor they might be involved in.

Even when there are less risky options to choose from, members of the risky group will prefer to take the highway of the risky choice. While we all engage in risky choices from time to time, those in this group are different from the occasional risky choice makers. They are different because making risky choices is as crucial to them as the oxygen they breathe. For them not to make a risky choice is like suffocating them. Their lives are more lively when they make risky choices.

The Selfish Group—There are two categories of people in this group and they are both in the business of watching out for their own interests:

- Detrimentally selfish group
- By the Book selfish group

Detrimentally selfish group: This selfish group is a group of people who make choices based on their selfish interests. They are always in the business of watching out for their own personal gain—even if it is to the detriment of others—they do not care.

For them, it all about what is in it for them. Their selfish interest is always their priority. This group of people can be found in every nook and cranny of the society. They don't care whom they trample upon in satisfying their quests. It does not matter to them who gets hurt in the process of acquiring their desires. All that matters to them is what is in it for them, and they will go to any length to achieve their selfish desires.

By the Book selfish group: This group of selfish people are selfish but not at the expense of others. In their dealings with others, they are watching out for their personal interests and, likewise, watching out for the interests of those they are dealing with. They are kind of selfish in the sense that they are putting themselves first, but not to hurt or harm of others. They might have their own interests at heart, but they will always play by the book, that is, sticking by the rules of the game.

The Survivor Group—The challenges of life do not have a timetable neither do they send a notice. At one stage or another, we all have been confronted with situations and happenings that compelled us to make choices to keep us afloat amid the challenges. The survivor group has made choices based on the circumstances and situations of life that confront them. Their choices are channeled to tackle and confront issues in the moment.

Often, their primary concern is to stay afloat in the midst of challenging situations. The choices they make amid challenges might not be the best choices, based on the prevailing situation, their choices are oriented towards survival. Their choices act as bridges that they use to cross over the troubling waters of life.

The Shadow Group—This is the group of people who make choices based on the choices of others. They end up walking in the light of the choices of others. In other words, they make choices based on what is popular.

They are the group who are always in the shadow of others. They are easily carried about by the wind and current of the popular choices. They always concur with others and mortgage their power of choice to others. They are the floating group in the Maze of Choices and they always agree to the choices of others, even when it is detrimental to them. This group of people have no roots of their own. They are easily carried away by the winds that blow through their lives.

CHOICES ARE FORERUNNERS

The Thoughtful Group—This group represent deep thinkers who engage their minds before making choices. They tap deeply into their powers of thought before making any choice and they weigh the pros and cons. Regardless, if they might be learned or unlearned, they are good at applying their power of thought in making choices. They are good in engaging their thoughts positively to steer their lives toward the direction that is profitable to themselves and others.

They are aware and conscious of the fact that choices carry an element of reward or punishment. They know that choices have implications. They are careful and deliberate in their choices and make choices thoughtfully.

They think it through first before making choices. They seek out knowledge in a particular area to gain insight that will empower them to make good choices. This does not mean they always make the perfect choice all the time, but they do not abuse or misuse or relegate their power of choice. They are fully aware that life is governed by choices; hence, they engage their power to choose positively.

Ultimately, regardless of the group we might be in within the Maze of Choices, the truth is we will live by our choices. It is very vital to engrave in our hearts that our choices are our forerunners. They go ahead of us into our future and await our arrival to determine our rewards or punishments based on our choices.

> There is power in the choices we make to initiate change. which can be permanent, temporary, or eternal changes, depending on what our choices entail.

CHAPTER 9

THE JOURNEY OF CHOICES

LIFE IS A journey and a race. The key elements that will determine how we fair in this journey are the choices we make in different chapters and phases of our lives. Living a life of relevance and influence is only attainable based on the choices we make, and the choices we make play major roles in orchestrating our relevance and influence in any spheres of life. The choices we make are the key elements that act as propellers for the actualization and fulfillment of our dreams and goals in life.

There is always a gap between our dreams and our realities, and the only thing that can fill that gap are the choices we make daily. All of our activities as human beings begin with making choices. Choice-making is the starting point of all the transactions in the streets of life. Navigating the Maze of Choices is the beginning of a new journey and most of the time, it is a journey that triggers a new chapter in our lives. The beginning of a new phase that usually does not reveal the end results until the journey is complete.

In the Maze of Choices, our choices can be embedded with opportunities, possibilities, prospects, successes, or failures, and the choices we make can become our cornerstones or stumbling blocks for our lives. In most aspects of life, we are confronted with options to choose from and whatever we choose propels our realities. Every choice we make at any given aspect of life has the power to be our forerunner and pathfinder in orchestrating our realities in the area where we make the choices.

The choices we make create our realities in all spheres of life.

The Pathway of Choices

In life's journey, a myriad of choices is presented in different spheres of life. Each of these choices we make automatically sets each and every one of us on a path in life. As we journey through the routes that our choices have placed us on, at different points on the journey, the need to make additional choices to smooth or roughen the journey becomes mandatory.

Each of these choices we make sets a wheel in motion in our lives, which will eventually attract more choices because choice never walks alone. Choice always attracts more choices, and every new choice we make in life's journey is being laid upon the previous choice made in the past.

The outcome of the choices we make cannot be totally articulated or predicted; hence, there is always need for us to make new choices until our choices come full circle. As we journey through the path our choices have placed us, the outcome might not be known. We might have a glimpse of the destination based on our experiences and encounters along the way, while in some situations we might be in total oblivion due to ignorance.

Therefore, every choice we make acts as a forerunner that prepare thes way for us to determine the smoothness or roughness of our journeys. Our choices are our messenger, announcer, and receptionist at every point in life. Whatever our experiences are in life, our life reflects the choices we've made.

THE JOURNEY OF CHOICES

The choices we make determine the kind of responses we get and the positions we occupy in life. We can be pioneers, trendsetters, trailblazer, follower, spectators, or people just existing instead of living and enjoying life to the fullest.

The choices we make in different areas of our lives have the power to become recurring decimals in our lives that will either work for our good or downfall. Therefore, the choices we make are either working for us or working against us.

Choices Are Forerunners

In the streets of life, the choices we make determine the transactions that take place in our lives.

One of the most common errors most of us, if not all of us, make is believing that the choices we make just end at the place where we made the choice or choices. Most of us have not realized that the choices we make every day in different areas of our lives do not just disappear or evaporate into the air. Instead, they go ahead of us as our forerunners to prepare and pave a path for us.

In life, every choice we make acts as our forerunners and pathfinders in the given area where the choice has been made. Our choices go ahead of us and wait for our arrival to determine the kind of reception we will receive. Hence, the choices of the past are still in effect, even when the choices were made a couple of years, days, or even a few seconds ago.

When a choice is made in any area of life, it does not just disappear, or go into extinction. Rather, it remains active and sometimes dormant until the set time where a situation or happening in our lives triggers it to become active. Once a choice is made in any given area of life, it transcends into our futures, to influence and determine the events and happenings that transpires in our lives. It becomes the foundation block in our lives that determines the level of stardom we attain in life.

CHOICES ARE FORERUNNERS

The choices we make are powerful because they have the power to stalk, intimidate, and harass us. On the other hand, our choices can become bridges we can rely on to cross troubled waters of life. They can also be a solid foundation upon which all the things that transpire in our lives are being built.

In the streets of life, our choices determine the transactions that take place in our lives. The choices we make in different areas of our lives have the power to become recurring decimals in our lives that will work for our good or downfall. Therefore, the choices we make are either working for us or against us. They have the power to become harassers, liabilities, obstacles, or the springboards and the masters of ceremony that announce us to our world.

Whatever choice we make, per time and situation, is positioning us for a reward or punishment, honor or dishonor, acceptance or rejection. Our choices can place us in a positive or negative light and have the power to transmit news waves into our lives. The choices we make in different aspects of our lives always act as our forerunners to pave a way for our arrivals, which eventually determine the kind of reception we will receive because the choices we made set the pedestal for our recognition for honor or dishonor, acceptance or rejection, reward or punishment.

The choices of today are the forerunners that go ahead of us to trigger the happenings, events, and transactions that will transpire in our futures. Whatever transpires in our future will be determined by the choices we make today, because life is lived based on the choices we make.

Just as the moon follows the pull of the earth around the sun to shine, that is how the choices we make align us to success or failure. Our choices are directly or indirectly aligning us with something.

Choices as Forerunner for Honor or Dishonor: Our past choices have the ability to rise over us like the sun to make us glow and shine.

Likewise, our choices have the power to cast a shadow over our lives like a cloud over us. The choices we make in life sum up to create the happenings and conditions in our lives. The choices we make personally and collectively pave a way for us to receive certain accolades in life; especially when the choices made have the elements that distinguish us to be recognized for good deeds that are beneficial to humanity.

On the flip side, when our choices entail evil deeds, it will certainly attract dishonor to our lives. In the Maze of Choices, the choices we make become our forerunners that go ahead of us to either bring us honor or dishonor.

Choices as Forerunner for Acceptance or Rejection: In any sphere in life, our ability to be receptive to others is about making choices, and these choices we have to make both on individual and collective levels. The choices we make personally or collectively pave a way for us to be accepted into a certain group or position in life. While there are cases where our choices have no relevancy to our acceptance but strictly depend on the choices of other people.

In the realms of acceptance and rejection, our choices and the choices of others determine our inclusiveness or marginalization. Although the choices other people make might stagnate or accelerate us in life's journey, but the choices we make personally in any sphere of life are active determinants in promoting our acceptance or rejection. Whatever frequency we might be operating from, our choices have the power to alter the course of our lives.

Choices as Forerunner for Reward or Punishment: We all make choices in different areas of life, and these choices we've made, whether on a personal level or as a group, differentiate us from others.

Our choices determine our results and what we attract into our lives. Prior choices are the propellers of today's results and they also determine the inscription on our emblems, whether they are rewards or punishments. The choices we make in different spheres of life are the ink which we and others around us use to inscribe our rewards or punishments in all spheres of life.

The choices we make have the inherent power to bring us rewards in the area of life where we have used our power of choice positively. Likewise, the choices we make can become avenues that attract punishment into our lives. It all depends on what our choices entail.

Ultimately, each and every one of us is solemnly responsible for our own choices because we are the custodians of our choices. Therefore, our lot in life is determined by the choices we make whether we are being rewarded or punished. In all affairs of life, we live our lives based on the combination of the choices we made.

Life Is Lived Based on a Combination of Choices

Life is lived based on the combination of the choices we make. The combination of our choices paints the portraits of our lives and maps out our destinies. The things we see as priorities in our lives are the things we focus on and are seen in the choices we make. The choices we make in different areas of our lives comes together to make and create the big things in our lives. All our choices in different endeavors of life are collected as pebbles that construct and decorate our lives.

Our choices are the building blocks that we use to build our lives. No matter how little or insignificant the choices we make in different areas of life might seem to be, they have the power to connect the different dots in our lives. When these dots are not appropriately connected, there might be a broken link which might incapacitate other areas of our lives. Our choices in all affairs of life call the shots in our lives.

Our choices in life will eventually determine our paths in life. In the Maze of Choices, our choices are leading us to a destination and, most times, the destination is unknown—this is the irony of the journey of choices. Most successful people in their various fields couldn't initially envision the magnitude of the success they now have when they made the choice to succeed in their various endeavors. Likewise, people who've made poor choices in different areas of their lives never knew the bad consequences the choices they made in the past would have on their futures and the futures of others.

The choices we make in all spheres of life are the dominant voices that will always speak into our lives and, to some extent, into the lives of others.

It is crucial not to take our freedom to choose for granted, because the choices we make in all spheres of life are the dominant voices that will always speaks into our lives and, to some extent, in the lives of others, especially those who are under our authorities, in our paths, and directly or indirectly connected to us, depending on our relationship, proximity, position, and authority in their lives. Just as the choices we make are the dominant voices that speak in our lives, and sometimes in the lives of others close to us, they are also the connectors that connects us with our dreams, goals, and purposes in life.

The choices we make today act as our connectors that connect us to our dreams and purposes in life.

Choices Are Connectors

Just as the choices we make are the dominant voices that speak in our lives, the choices we make today act as our connector that connects us to our dreams and purpose in life. Our choices connect us to next stages and phases in our lives. They connect the dots between our dreams, goals, and purposes in life. Therefore, the choices we make individually or collectively go ahead of us into our tomorrows as connectors, to connect each one of us to what the choices made in the past had birthed or produce in our lives.

Our outcomes in life, locations, and situations today were orchestrated by the choices we made in the past.

CHOICES ARE FORERUNNERS

Whatever we will attain in life begins with the choices we make. Choice-making is the starting point in attaining and fulfilling any goal in life. In all affairs of life, our choices act as bridges, that connect us from the place of desiring to the place of actualizing our dreams. The choices we make in different spheres of our lives are the links that connect our todays with our tomorrows. They determine if our tomorrows will be better than today. Having a more fruitful, productive, and colorful tomorrow begins with making good, right, and just choices. Whatever transpires in our tomorrows is at the mercy of the choices we make today.

Our choices can become the source of our fulfillment or defeat in life.

Our Choices Are a Launching Pad

Every endeavor and activity in life begins with a choice. The choices we make in different areas set in motion all transactions that transpire in our lives—the choices we make get the ball rolling in the affairs of life. Despite the oppositions, oppressions, and unfavorable conditions of life, our choices have the power to create opportunities that pave a way for us to triumph and succeed in life. Therefore, our successes or failures, defeats or victories in life are incubated in the choices we make in different areas of our lives.

Our choices are the launch pad that triggers the series of events that transpire in our lives. In one area of our lives or another, we are daily engaging our power of choice and all the choices we make become the launch pad that initiates the changes and transactions that transpire in our lives. The choices we make in different areas of our lives are being summed into events and eventualities in our lives that determine our positions and outcomes in all affairs of life.

Our choices act as a launch pad for our successes or failures, triumphs or defeats, conquering or being conquered. Whatever transpires in our lives is being orchestrated by the choices we make and sometimes by the choices, others make with or without our consent.

THE JOURNEY OF CHOICES

The choices we make individually or collectively as a group are the initiators of all transactions that take place in our lives.

Choices Position and Reposition

The positions in which we find ourselves in life are determined by the choices we make. Outside the pre-conditions we were born with, the divinely orchestrated places where we were born, the family and race we are born into, all other aspects of our lives, in terms of growth, development, and healthy living depend on the choices we make. Our choices in different areas of our lives determine our positions and locations at different points in life's journey. The positions we all occupy in life are at the mercies of our choices.

Our choices determine the realm we will operate in because the choices we make have the power to position us in different realms in life. They have the power to place us in the realms of stability or uncertainty. Wrong choices lead to wrong steps, which create wrong and unpleasant outcomes. These unpleasant outcomes can only be changed by making better choices that will reverse the wrong choices that were made in the past. Our locations, positioning, and repositioning in life are determined by our choices, which will eventually influence what we can access and what can access us.

Every unpleasant situation and circumstance can be turned around or changed by the choices we will make amid the prevailing circumstance or situation. Our choices eventually reposition us in the desired realm. Every junction of choice-making is a place of calculating and recalculating for repositioning in the desired realm we want to be in life.

> *The choices we make have the power to determine our positions and locations in life. Our choices are always directly or indirectly aligning us with something.*

Our choices have the power to position us as front liners, pioneers, trendsetters, and trailblazers. They position us for opportunities that will change and upgrade our lives or that will oppose us from getting useful opportunities that would have enhance our lives.

Choices Determine Location—Our choices are our modes of transportation we use to journey and sail through life. They determine how buoyant, smooth, and peaceful our journeys are. The choices we make at different spheres of life are our navigators in life's journey. They navigate our daily activities, whether we are aware of it or not.

Our choices determine our location at any given point in time. If peradventure, we are not satisfied with our present location in life, then the choices we will make amid the present situation can change our location to the desired location.

Of course, other factors might influence our ability to relocate, but the major influencers are our choices. The choices we make will aid in appropriating other factors that might be obstacles to align with our goal to ensure that the desired outcome is actualized.

Our location might act as a hindrance to our dreams sometimes, but the choices we will make in our present location determine the changes that will transpire in our lives. Our choices transform a wilderness into fertile lands. For example, the tremendous transformation we all see in Dubai and her environs begins with the choice the people made to transform a desert into a world-class destination for tourists and business. Also, Malala Yousafzai made a choice that placed her on the world's stage as an influencer and a role model.

Wherever we are today and where we will be tomorrow is at the mercy of the choices we make. Our choices have the power to transform our present locations and transport us to our desired locations in the future.

Choices Nurture or Devour

The choices we all make daily don't only impact or affect us alone. They impact others around us and those we come in contact with. Our choices can become opportunities to nurture or devour ourselves and others. The choices we make can either nurture or devour different things in life, such as our peace, self-esteem, opportunities, and unity. It all depends on the path which we choose to take, especially if we always choose to see the imperfection in others and ourselves.

Any choice we make that exploits the weaknesses of others can either make them strive to be better or cause them to be in despair. The choices we make concerning others can make them to go the extra mile by striving to attain more or they make them give up. We can give others hope or despair, because our choices concerning them is either adding value to others or devaluing them. Our choices can catapult us and others to higher heights by adding value or they can do the opposite.

Our choices can nurture others not to give up but to believe in themselves or to throw in the towel. Our choices can be a lifeline to others. They do not only affect and influence our destinies but the destinies of others as well.

Choices Are an Individual and Collective Responsibility

In life, choices are made individually and collectively as a group. The effect and outcome of the choices we make, whether on an individual or collective level, can result in a profitable or detrimental outcome.

- *Collective* choices are choices we make on the basis of group agreement for the benefit or detrimental discomfort of all. Collective choices are made as a family, organization, community, and country. However, on the collective level, individuals in authority triggers the choices, which is eventually presented to other people in the group for their consent and approval.

    Once the choice is approved by the group, it becomes a collective choice with the backing of the group. Also, a collective choice can be triggered by an individual in a group, who is not an authority figure but has followers within the organization, family, or community.

That is why the forming of cartels and cabals are vital in making a collective choice. Collective choices are mostly anchored on intent, which can be for service or selfish reasons.

- *Individual* choices are mostly made on an individual level either with or without the consent of others. These choices enhance personal well-being and sometimes the well-being of others. On the other hand, they can also be choices made to harm and hurt others, knowingly or unknowingly. As such, they also harm and hurt the one making the choices.

Both collective and individual choices foster something in our lives and in the lives of others.

Most times life presents us with the opportunity to choose which path we want to embark on. Our choices can become a place of fighting or surrendering, conquering or being conquered, victory or defeat. Hence, our choices foster something in our lives.

The Choices We Make Foster Something in Our Lives

Our choices in different spheres of our lives foster good and bad things in our lives. Every choice we make can either profit or cost us something, which can have a positive or negative impact in our lives and the lives of others around us.

There is power in the choices we make to initiate change, which can be permanent, temporary, or eternal change. Some of our choices might cause temporary discomfort initially before giving birth to a lifetime of bliss. Some choices we make might result in a short-term gratification, but eventually, in the long run, result in pain and sorrow.

In the realm of relationships, our good choices can foster peace and stability of our relationships, while poor financial choices can foster

THE JOURNEY OF CHOICES

financial discomfort and stress. Life can become a nightmare when our past choices interfere with our futures and hold us hostage.

When life present to us the opportunity to make choices in any area of life, it is crucial to be conscious of the fact that our choices will eventually foster something in our lives and in the lives of others. Whatever we do not want in our lives, we should not make the choices that will incubate and foster them to become a reality in our lives.

In the streets of life, the good, just, and right choices we make act as streetlights. They brighten and lighten our paths as we journey through life.

> *There are certain things in life we do not have control over, but there are still things in life we do have control over, and we can only control most things in life by the choices we make daily.*

CHAPTER 10

DETERMINANT OF CHOICES

IN ALL SPHERES of life, there are different things that serve as triggers to bring things into existence. In the Maze of Choices, certain things act as facilitators in the choices we make. These facilitators influence and propel our choices in different spectrums of life. Additionally, determinants of our choices are factors that influence the choices we make in different areas of life. These factors can be conflicting or empowering, and they have the power to influence our choices.

These factors known as determinants of choices act as triggers for the choices we make. However, we use reasons as a means to justify these determinants to favor our course whether individually or collectively as a group.

These reasons vary from one situation to another and from person to person; nevertheless, our choices have the power to set a wheel in motion in our lives. Unfortunately, the kind of wheel our choices set in motion might be beneficial or detrimental, depending on what the choices entail.

CHOICES ARE FORERUNNERS

The wheel that our choices set in motion corresponds with our intentions to ensure the realization of what our choices entail. Our intentions are major facilitators that works with other determinants to motivate our choices.

In the Maze of Choices, there are two determinants:

- Primary Determinant
- Secondary Determinants

In the Maze of Choices, we tend to blame the secondary determinants for the choices we make. Although the secondary determinants might act as a catalyst that facilitates and enforces our choices, the primary determinant at the end is the sole proprietor of our choices.

Below are some of the **secondary determinants** of choices:

- Association
- Assumption
- Belief and Conviction
- Character
- Desire
- Development
- Environment
- Finance
- Focus
- Health
- Hope
- Impatience
- Inner Conflict
- Intention

- Information/Knowledge
- Perception
- Perspective

Just as the moon gets light from the sun, that is how other people's choices reflect and rub on us due to our alignment and fraternization with them.

Association—The company we keep has the power to influence the choices we make. Any fraternity with any person or group of people has the power to build, derail, impact, implicate, impede, and influence our choices. We are never greater or better than the people we keep and continuously fraternize with. The associations we mingle with always transmit into our lives their characters and mentalities with or without our permission, as long as we are within the range of their transmission. The people in our lives have the power to influence our power of choice.

It is imperative for us to be intentional and selective of who we mingle with, because our associations can influence the choices we make. All of our associations either complete, complement, or hinder our progress and success in life.

A close and habitual association with someone who is negative will corrupt and influence the choices we make. Likewise, a close and habitual friendship with a positive thinker will motivate, impact, empower, and influence us to make good choices.

Our perception, perspective, progress, and success in life is directly influenced by our associations. Just as the Book of Proverbs says, those who walk with the wise will be wise and associate with fools and you will act foolishly. In other words, when we walk with those who make good choices, we will make good choices, but when we walk with those who make bad choices, we will make bad choices. Just as the moon gets light from the sun that is how other people's choices reflect and rub on us due to our association and fraternization with them. We must be selective of our associations.

> *Assumption can divert us and take us off track. This is because when we make assumptions, we do not possess adequate information or knowledge about a person or situation.*

Assumption—In the Maze of Choices, assumptions are a common determinant that can turn the course of any situation. Assumption in any of the affairs of life, where we lack knowledge, can influence the choices we make negatively, and this can be harmful and destructive.

In the Maze of Choices, assumptions have the power to fill the gaps with information that might be incorrect and that can have adverse effects on the choices we make. In any sphere of life, when we make choices based on assumptions, it affects our results.

When we choose the route of assumption instead of going for insight, we place limitations on our ability to develop our wisdom bank. Relying on our assumptions deprives us the privilege of learning new things that can enhance our abilities to make correct choices.

Assumptions are always antagonists to learning. They block the possibility of gaining important information or insight that might enhance the choices we make in any given situation. Anytime there is a missing puzzle in any given situation, our ability to have clarity is hampered when we are not aided with the right information.

Assumptions have the power to mislead, and they can become an avenue to fill in wrong information based on ignorance. On the other hand, assumption is sometimes rooted in arrogance, or in an unwillingness to learn from others or ask the right relevant questions. Whenever we choose to assume instead of asking questions, confusion is created, and a vacuum develops which can result in adverse and unpleasant outcomes.

DETERMINANT OF CHOICES

Assumption is a presumptuous behavior of not going outside one's box to search for facts that can influence and enhance our choices. Assumptions are the propeller that fills gaps with information that seems real to us in the Maze of Choices. They divert our journey and takes us off track, because we do not have adequate information or knowledge about a situation. Assumption will impede our ability to choose aright in any situation. Assumption can become a determining factor that decides the outcome of our choices.

Belief and Conviction—Our belief system is programmed by our environment, upbringing, and/or association, and they directly influence the choices we make in all areas of life.

Our belief is the baseline that engenders our conviction. While our conviction eventually affects and determines the choices that we make in different situations of life, our choices always align with our convictions.

Whenever we are in a position to make choices, the tendency to make choices that are in accordance with our belief overshadows other reasonable options that might be more profitable in that given situation or circumstance.

At various junctions in life, our choices can become the place of our imprisonment or freedom because of our belief. Sometimes, our beliefs and convictions have the power to determine if the choices we make are convicting or acquitting us. Our conviction in any situation inspires and controls the choices we make.

> ***The company we keep affects our character and our character influences the choices we make.***

Character—Character is the real and authentic version of you. Our character is seen through our collective qualities, such as our moral and mental attributes that distinguish each one of us from another via the agency of our behavior and lifestyle.

Our moral and mental attributes are exhibited and transmitted via the choices we make and through our actions and dealings with others. Our character transmits who we truly are and is reflected in the choices we make. Our choices have a way of catching up with us to bear witness of our character without our permission.

In the race of life, people are quick to invest more in their reputation than their character to deceive others. This, to some extent, might work for a while but in the end, their choices reveal their true character.

No matter how hard we try to invest in our reputation to mislead others, the choices we make have a way of revealing our true character. There is a way our character always surfaces and taints our reputational investment because our characters are radiative in nature and the choices, we make are reflections of our character.

Choices are tools, we use to create the futures we desire and do not desire.

Desire—Desire is a major determinant in the Maze of Choices, and it has the power to command and control the choices we make in all walks of life. Desire is the flame that kindles the fire of possibilities in the race of life.

In all spheres of life, our desires control our focus and influence the choices we make, while the choices we make in different affairs of our lives are incubated by our desires. Our desires are incubators for the choices we make.

Every attainment in life is triggered by desire. Our desires influence the choices we will make, and, in turn, our choices reflect our desires.

In most realms of life, we base our choices on our desires; therefore, any choice we make in any area of life aligns with our desires. Desire is a determinant in the Maze of Choice; however, the choices we make, and their outcome depends on the force fanning our desires.

DETERMINANT OF CHOICES

Our developmental growth in any area of life enhances our abilities to make good, right, and just choices.

Development—In all walks of life, our personal development affects our capacity. Therefore, our developmental capacity determines what we can attempt and do in life, which also affects the choices we make.

Development is a broad word, which covers different aspects of life; the depth of our emotional, educational, financial, mental, physical, social, or spiritual development affects and influences the choices we make in different issues of life. That is why different people in a similar situation make different choices. It is because their development and strength are different from each other.

Our development is a dominant factor that contributes immensely in, orchestrating our choices. Our maturity in any given area of life determines the choices we will make regarding issues that might arise.

The depth of our development is a determinant that places an invisible or visible bar on us, which directly and indirectly influences the choices we make. The more matured and developed we are in the developmental scale, the more responsibilities we have and the higher the expectations of others from us. These responsibilities and expectations directly influence and control the choices we make in any given situation or circumstance. Our developmental depth places us in a class which continuously controls our choices.

Environment—Our environment affects and influences our choices. The influence and effect of our environment or background cannot be underestimated, because the influence of our environment is seen in the choices we make. Our environment directly and indirectly controls our choices, and our environment has the power to program and control our lives via the agency of the choices we make, which eventually impacts our progress in life.

Our environments and backgrounds control our belief systems, perspectives, and perceptions of life, and our beliefs, perspectives, and perceptions influence the choices we make. Our environment has a way of programming and influencing our choices. This eventually determines our lifestyles and the paths we take in life. Our environment sets the standard for the choices we make, and these choices control our way of life. In life, our choices act as the measuring gauge that determines our experiences, outcomes, and results in life.

Our environments have the power to govern the choices we make, while the choices we make create our experiences and the events that transpire in our lives. Our environments have the power to influence us positively or negatively. The influence of our environments on us is seen in the choices we make in different areas of our lives. Ultimately, our environments have the power to map and control our futures through the choices that we make.

Finance—Our financial status in life has the power to control and influence the choices we make. Our financial strength has a way of slipping into our consciences to control our perspectives and perceptions of life. These directly and indirectly influence the choices we make socially, mentally, spiritually, and in our relationships and general well-being.

Our financial status consciously and subconsciously controls our dealings between ourselves and others around us. Our financial status can be a blessing by empowering us to make choices that will bless and empower humanity, or our financial background can be a thorn in the flesh when we make choices that become an instrument to hurt ourselves or belittle others.

Directly or indirectly, our position on the financial ladder is a common determinant that influences our choices. Because our position on the financial ladder has the power to make us and others the victims of our choices, it is imperative to have a sort of check and balance in your life to keep you from being intoxicated by your financial affluence.

DETERMINANT OF CHOICES

Focus—Our focus influences our choices. In all spheres of life, whatever captures our attention controls our focus and influences our choices. Likewise, whatever we surround ourselves with can also control our focus, which eventually controls the choices we make. Our surroundings, happenings, experiences, and the people in our lives have the ability to control our focus and influence our power of choice.

Our aspirations and the events that transpire in our lives are determined by what we focus on, while our focus is unequivocally controlled by our environment and the people in our lives. In order to make good choices in different areas of our lives, we must control what accesses our lives; because whatever can access our lives can control our focus.

Our focus determines the transactions that take place in our lives and influences the choices we make in different affairs of life. Our focus eventually determines our chances, opportunities, possibilities, and what we will attain in life. Therefore, whatever we focus on is either stepping us up or pulling us back.

In life, we cannot achieve much without the force of focus. Focus is a major denominator in the equation of success and an active denominator in our decision-making. Even when we make choices on the spur of the moment, the choices we make are still triggered by a subconscious interest we focused on in the past. In all areas of life, our focus has the power to propel the choices we make.

Health—Our state and condition in terms of health affects and determines the choices we make. The choices we make in different realms of our lives can be propelled by our health awareness and medical conditions. Our medical conditions are major determinants that can influence the choices we make in different issues of life. Our medical conditions control all aspects of our lives and the choices we make in all spheres of life.

CHOICES ARE FORERUNNERS

Our hope is the fuel that keeps the flames of our desires and expectations alive in all spheres of life.

Hope—Hope is a key factor in keeping us afloat amid life's challenges. it is a propeller that enhance decision-making in all spheres of life. Hope is a force and anchor in the Maze of Choice. Hope is a force and lifeline that upholds and sustains us in impossible situations. It is the force of hope that makes us keep going when everything around us screams it is over.

The force of hope is a determinant in decision-making. Having hope amid life challenges strengthens us to make choices that empower us to sail through the storms of life. Having hope is what keeps us going through the various dark tunnels of life. It helps us keep believing that there will be a ray of light at the end of the tunnel during our hour of trials.

The force of hope tells us that there are new possibilities and opportunities in every day. Hope is what makes it possible to make choices that will make the sun to shine in various challenges.

It takes hope to make tough choices amid life's challenges. Having hope keeps us from give up. The choices we make in different areas of our lives exhibit and showcase the tenacity of our hope.

Impatience—Impatience is a subtle determinant that pushes people to make choices that can be detrimental to them and others. In the race of life, our desires to have results at the speed of light can make us make choices that are harmful to us and other people around us.

Impatience can have positive and negative vibes because impatience is like a two-sided sword that can be a weapon of defense or destruction.

In the Maze of Choices, impatience can have adverse and profitable effects, depending on your perspective. For example, being impatient with the lifestyle of mediocracy triggers choices that will bring

DETERMINANT OF CHOICES

about positive change. Whereas greed is another factor that exhibits or showcases the negative side of impatience.

In the Maze of Choices, impatience is a determinant that influences our choices. Impatience can be positive or negative determinants, depending on the intent and the force propelling our choices.

Intention—There is always a purpose, a reason behind the choices we make in different areas of life. Our purpose is a driving force that determines our choices. In the Maze of Choices, intention is a propelling force that helps to facilitate our choices.

Our intentions are expressed outwardly via the choices we make. Most transactions in the streets of life are being orchestrated by the intent of our hearts. Our intentions then control and affect our choices. Our intentions can be good, kind, and gracious, or bad, evil, and wicked. No matter what our intentions are, our choices will align and reflect our intentions.

In all spheres of life, the choices we make showcase our intentions and the states of our hearts. Every choice we make is conceived with an inner intent and purpose.

Inner Conflict / Peace—Our internal state is a key factor that influences our choices. Whatever transpires in us internally controls the choices we make about issues in our lives and concerning those around us. We cannot separate our inner state from our choices. When we are internally at peace, it reflects in the choices we make. Where there is instability, insecurity, hatred, rancor, and/or jealousy, our choices will align with what is prevailing internally.

Inner-conflict' leads to choices that reflect conflict and chaos. When there is peace, tranquility, joy, and calmness internally, our choices will reflect those states.

Knowledge and ignorance; actively influence our choices.

Information and Knowledge—In life, there is always missing information or a puzzle that cannot be put together. This impedes our choices until the appropriate information and missing link are known. Hence, the appropriate application of information and knowledge are strong determinant in the Maze of Choices.

We make choices based on the knowledge available to us, and the insight we have about a specific topic or issue influences the choices that we make regarding any particular situation. Choices are easily made when we have knowledge or information about a situation or circumstance. The application of knowledge is vital in order to avert making poor or bad choices that can lead to regrets. It is wise to acquire knowledge before making choices in any issue because a positive foreknowledge, and an in-depth insight, and a wise application of the knowledge helps us to make right, just, and good choices. Ultimately, the depth of our knowledge in any sphere of life gives us an edge and broadens our horizons.

Perception—Sometimes in life we choose certain options based on our understanding and interpretation of the situation and the way we interpret information, situations, or events affects and propels the choices we make.

Perception can be negative or positive. Negative perception is deceptive. Having a negative perception about a person, situation, or things can crowd our abilities to choose rightly; while positive perceptions enhance our abilities to choose rightly. Either way, the negative and positive perceptions have the power to influence the choices we make in all realms of life.

> ***Our choices are outlets through which our perception is revealed.***

Our ability to understand and interpret situations, things, and happenings in our lives is anchored on our mental well-being. Therefore, our capability to analyze, process, or understand information, situations, or things depends on our internal states, which eventually expresses itself externally.

Our perception is expressed externally through the choices we make. Both our internal and external states directly and indirectly control the choices we make. Every choice reveals our perceptions about a person, piece of information, situation, happening, or event. Our choices are outlets through which our perceptions are revealed.

Perspective—Our perspective is the way we see things, and it is a determinant that influences our choices. In affairs of life, our perspectives determine our responses or reactions to issues. A wrong perspective can impede our choices, while a right perspective can bring clarity and enhance our ability to choose correctly in a given situation.

Our ability to choose rightly depends on the information we assimilate. Information fuels our perspective, and our perspective influences our opinion. Our opinions have ways of interfering with the choices we make concerning an individual, organization, people, thing, and situation.

Ultimately, all the secondary determinants of choices are interwoven. They are like tentacles in our lives that engender and facilitate our choices.

A choice has no power to make itself. We are the ones who make choices, and we are responsible for our choices. Therefore, we are individually and collectively the sole proprietors of the choices we make.

Primary Determinant of Choice

- **YOU (WE)**

You must refuse to be the victim of your own choices because you are the sole proprietor of your choices.

CHOICES ARE FORERUNNERS

YOU—Whiles secondary determinants influence the choices we make, no choices can be made without the primary determinant, which is **YOU** individually and **We,** collectively.

YOU and I are the common denominators in the Maze of Choices. We are the proprietors of the choices we make in spite of the secondary determinants.

We have to personally pull the choice trigger to make whatever choice we make because choice has no power to make itself. Of course, there might be conditions or situations that might be confrontational in our lives that are beyond our control, such as pre-conditions, circumstantial conditions, or health conditions.

Nevertheless, the choices we make amid these conditions have ways of influencing our outcomes and experiences in life. We are the ones who make choices, and we are responsible for the choices we make. We are the sole proprietors of the choices we make individually and collectively.

Although people and situations might amplify or act as catalysts to facilitate the choices we make. We are responsible for the choices we make because, when all is said and done, we are the custodians of the choices we make individually and collectively. We are the ones who set the choice wheel in motion in our lives irrespective of the secondary determinants.

The consequences or rewards of our choices are not transferable.

Our Choices Are Our Responsibilities

In as much as other factors act as catalysts in facilitating the choices, we make we are solemnly responsible for the choices we make. Taking ownership of our choices fosters a learning process that enhances our experiences, which empowers us to make right and good choices amid life's challenges.

DETERMINANT OF CHOICES

As much as we individually or collectively as a group want to transfer or blame others for the outcomes of bad, poor, or illicit choices we've made in the past, the fact is we cannot escape the consequences or rewards of the choices we make.

We cannot disown, reject, or separate ourselves from the choices we make. Refusing to take responsibility for the bad choices we make will only prolong our suffering, heartache, sorrow, and disappointments. Taking responsibility for our choices enhances our abilities to learn and to choose rightly when we face similar situations in the future.

> *We must consciously and intentionally choose rightly in order not to make ourselves and others the victims of the choices we make, because not all choices made can be undone.*

CHAPTER 11

OPERATIVE DIMENSIONS OF CHOICE

THE CHOICES WE make can express themselves in different dimensions—which can be positive or negative dimensions, depending on the outcomes they produce. Every choice we make has the power to express itself in different dimensions, depending on what the choice entails and the intention propelling the choice.

In the Maze of Choices, the dimensions in which the choices we make are operating are like breathing in oxygen and breathing out carbon dioxide. Good choices are comparable to taking in oxygen, which is the source of sustaining life and eventually birthing healthy outcomes. On the other hand, the poor, bad, or illicit choices we make can be likened to the process of taking in carbon dioxide, that leads to poisonous and deadly outcomes.

We all know that oxygen is crucial for our existence. Choices are just as vital to our lives, because they influence and determine what surges into our lives and what exits our lives.

The dimensions our choices operate in are translated into different experiences in our lives. Every good, just, and right choice we make will have a positive, impact in our lives and the lives of others. Wrong, poor, and bad choices are the sponsors of mistakes, errors, regrets, and heartaches in life. The truth is, all the choices we make, whether good, just, poor, or bad control the activities in the streets of life, and they express themselves in some of the dimensions below.

Operative Dimensions of Choices

- Blindfold Dimension
- Boldness Dimension
- Chain Reaction Dimension
- Chinese Bamboo Tree Dimension
- Dedication Dimension
- Deflation Dimension
- Disruptive Dimension
- Domino Effect Dimension
- Doppler Effect Dimension
- Droste Effect Dimension
- Halo Effect Dimension
- Instruction Dimension
- Intention Dimension
- Irritation Dimension
- The Past Dimension
- Planning Dimension
- Priority Dimension
- Procrastination Dimension
- Profit Dimension

OPERATIVE DIMENSIONS OF CHOICE

- Question and Answer Dimension
- Ripple Effect Dimension
- Sinkhole Dimension
- Soul Dimension
- Thermometer and Thermostat Dimension
- Thought Dimension
- Value Dimension
- Weapon Dimension
- Word Dimension

Blindfold Dimension—In the Maze of Choices, none of us can fully predict the outcomes of the choices we make. Despite our brains working to envision the outcomes of the choices we make it is absolutely impossible to see the end from the beginning. This is a dilemma we as humans encounter in the Maze of Choices. The choices we make are similar to a blindfold process where we cannot see or predict the absolute outcomes of the choices we make.

In the Maze of Choices, there is always the possibility of being blindfolded. The blindfold operative dimension of choices is actively in operation in the Maze of Choices because a choice might seem right, good, or perfect, but the outcome might be destructive.

Assumption, limited information, and ignorance are active forces that make us blind to the outcomes of our choices. Therefore, assumption, limited information about an issue, and ignorance are deadly companions in the Maze of Choices that can sabotage and impede our abilities to make the right, good, and perfect choices.

Assumption, limited information, lack of understanding, and ignorance are the catalysts that propel the blindfold dimensions into effect. Whenever we act on assumption, limited information, or ignorance, and not on facts, the possibility of making poor or bad choices is maximized, while the possibility of making good and just choices is minimized. The outcomes of such choices can have grievous effects on us and others.

Boldness Dimension—The race of life entails risk-taking and the Maze of Choices are mazes of adventure. It takes boldness to embark on it. Every endeavor is attainable based on our willingness to take calculated risks.

In all spheres of life, our successes and attainments are at the mercies of our level of boldness. In the race of life, boldness is an operative dimension that is crucial for determining our success in all areas of life. Whatever we can accomplish in life is orchestrated by the choices we make, and it takes boldness to make certain choices.

Boldness is a vital mentality needed in the race of life. When we are bold it is by choice. Boldness is an operative dimension in the Maze of Choices that fuels our desire to achieve and dare what others fear or think is impossible.

Boldness is the platform in the Maze of Choices that supports the attainment of new heights and statuses in all spheres of life. No one can attain anything in life without engaging the force of boldness. We might have a dream, a goal, or a desire; however, it takes boldness to make the choices that will make them a reality.

There is absolutely no endeavor in life that does not require boldness to become a reality or materialize. Our attainment or accomplishment in any field is anchored on how bold we are to get it. Our success tomorrow depends on what we dare to confront or contend with today. We can use boldness in the race of life to succeed and attain success.

New choices strengthen, enforce, or dismantle existing, choices, which can result in a chain reaction.

OPERATIVE DIMENSIONS OF CHOICE

Chain Reaction Dimension—A set of related choices made in any given area of life has the power to produce reactions and outcomes in different areas of our lives. A chain reaction is an operative dimension in the Maze of Choices because the choices we make are catalysts that can cause chain reactions.

The choices we make in one area of life can create a chain reaction that will expand to other areas of our lives and sometimes into the lives of others who are at the epicenter and within the circumference of the choice we make.

Our choices can provoke a chain reaction that creates a continuous circle of events that trigger more choices. The chain reaction operative dimension of choice can create a virtuous or vicious circle in our lives and in the lives of others, depending on what the choices we make entail.

The choices we make in all spheres of life are embedded with the power to create and engineer a chain reaction, which can be beneficial or destructive. Knowing the potentiality each choice can have in creating and engineering a chain reaction in our lives and the lives of others is essential to making beneficial choices.

Our inner instinct or witness are like the red and yellow traffic signals that warn us on how to make decisions and protect us from negative chain reactions.

The Chinese Bamboo Tree Dimension—As human beings, some choices we make are like the Chinese bamboo tree, which contain in it two dimensions. The dimensions of hope and warning. The dimension of hope tells us not to give up making good choices even when there is delayed gratification. The dimension of warning tells us that there is a day of recompense and ramification for the illicit, ill, and wicked choices we make.

In the Maze of Choices, some choices we make exhibit the characteristics of the Chinese bamboo tree, which lies dormant for years without any major sign of growth but later exhibits an exponential growth in a very short time the fifth year. That is how some of the choices we make in different aspects of life are. The effects and outcome of our choices might not be seen immediately, but eventually their impact slips in and shows itself in different areas in our lives

Since some of the choices we make exhibit the Chinese bamboo tree characteristics of not having immediate or instant gratification or ramification, we continue to engage in making choices that can be beneficial or destructive to us and others.

Just as the Chinese bamboo tree completes its growth circle at the appointed time, our choices in life might be dormant for a while; but will produce an outcome and happenings in our lives at the appointed time once the wheel of choices has been set in motion. The choices we make will always birth what it entails in our lives and the lives of others, in greater and deeper dimensions, because choices are not defunct but extant in nature.

Dedication Dimension—The dedication operative dimension of choices is a dimension in the Maze of Choices, where our dedication and commitment to a course, assignment, and/or responsibility controls the choices we make and the actions we take.

In all aspects of life, our commitment as a person or a group to an organization, a community, or duty influences the choices we make per time and situation. It is a realm in the Maze of Choices where our commitment to a course became a zeal that envelops all our focus in every facet of life.

The dedication dimension of choices reflects our commitment to different courses in life. It is a dimension of being committed to a course which ensures that the course can be achieved, irrespective of the oppositions or circumstances that might try to be hindrances. Our commitment is a force that enhances and strengthens our choices.

OPERATIVE DIMENSIONS OF CHOICE

In this dimension we individually or collectively make the choice to devote and invest our time, energy, or resources to a purpose for the betterment of ourselves and others. It is a dimension of self-sacrifice to a given course, where we are willing to sacrifice something for a better future. It is a realm in the Maze of Choices where the choices we make cost us something directly or indirectly.

Being dedicated to a goal or course, entails hard work to deliver the expected or desired result. Dedication determines and influences our standard for living. In the Maze of Choices, whenever we engage the force of dedication to a course or an agenda, our results are undeniably outstanding because dedication is reflective just as choices are reflective.

Deflation Dimension—Deflation is a word synonymous with economics and the erosion of soil by wind and water. In the Maze of Choices, the deflation dimension of choices is actively in operation. This is where the bad or poor choices we make, or others make on our behalf, over a period of time in the same direction dehumanize us as humans and erode opportunities in our lives. That is the essence of the deflation dimension. It is a major sponsor of stagnation, problems, and chaos in the streets of life.

On the other hand, the deflation dimension of choices can have a positive vibe in it, especially when we choose to deflate certain incidents or bad patterns in our lives, communities, or society. This results in peace and stability. Likewise, when we make the right choice to deflate certain ancient patterns or behaviors of operations that have been draining our peace and attacking our unity and finances, we will experience a tremendous growth.

In the Maze of Choices, the deflation dimension of choices either slows us down or increases our growth. Every day, when we engage our power of choice positively, we experience growth. On the flip side, when we engage our power of choice negatively, we cause erosion in our lives and experience decrease in our growth.

The deflation dimension of choices either place us and others in an advantageous or disadvantageous position. This is because the deflation dimension of choices always results in increasing or decreasing, upgrading or downgrading our potentials and opportunities in all realms of life.

Disruptive Dimension—Our choices can be disruptive in nature, since life is lived based on the compilations of the choices, we make. The disruptive dimension of choices disrupts the norm and status quo to bring about change, which can have a positive or negative outcome.

Some disruptive choices can be empowering or disarming; it all depends on what the choices we make entail. Most times, the word "disruptive" has negative connotations to it. Yet sometimes the disruptive dimension of choices can bring us positive results; especially when we engage the disruptive dimension of choices to initiate a positive change in an area of our lives.

When certain positive changes occur because we choose to disrupt the existing norm, the outcomes can outweigh the inconveniences the choice might cause. For example, when we individually or collectively as a group make the choice to disrupt the lifestyle of mediocrity, we will experience a tremendous growth in our lives.

On the other hand, the disruptive operative dimension of choices has an inherent power to turn the world of an individual or a group upside down, especially when we choose to conduct or engage ourselves in an illicit, dangerous endeavor that can be detrimental to our lives and the lives of others. The disruptive operating dimension of choices can be positively or negatively disruptive. It all depends on what our choices entail.

> ***The choices we make have a lot of recipients; that is why the choices of another person can have a profitable or devastating domino effect on a family, community, company, country, or the world.***

OPERATIVE DIMENSIONS OF CHOICE

Domino Effect Dimension—Often we cannot envision the cumulative effect of our choices until such effects have taken place. Most of the time the cumulative effects of our choices merely remain eventualities until they come to pass.

While the domino effect dimension of choices has a starting time, sometimes it is difficult to ascertain the end point. The domino effect dimension occurs in the Maze of Choices when a choice made by an individual, a parent, an organization, and/or government initiates a succession of events that cut across the board to impact those who are in the path of the choice.

The domino effect dimension of choices shows how delicate choices are in influencing, molding, shaping, and affecting the general well-being of every one of us as human beings.

The domino effect dimension of choice can be positive or negative. Most times, the domino effect dimension of choice is synonymous with negative outcome, however, the domino effect dimension can also carry with it an element of positivity, depending on the choices we make.

That is why when we as individuals are privileged to occupy a position or office where the lives of others are being influenced by our choices, it is crucial to known and remember that the destinies of those in our care are in our hands. Every single choice we make, whether good or bad, will affect, influence, and/or reroute the lives of others and their outcomes in life.

Whether we are parents, executives, teachers, doctors, or in the governing council, it is vital we make choices that will not derail or hinder us individually and those that are under our care because any choice we make can have a domino effect in our lives and in the lives of those under our care.

When a leader makes good and just choices on behalf of those under his or her care, it will result in a positive domino effect. On the other hand, if the choice is bad, it will have a negative domino effect. This is the reality we all are living in every day, where the choices of others have the power to produce, positive or negative domino effects in our lives.

Our choices and the choices of others have the inherent power to control the affairs of our lives and determine our outcomes in life.

Doppler Effect Dimension—The choices we make create different effects and outcomes in our lives and the lives of others around us. Just as the choices people make vary from one person to another, the outcomes have different effects on us and those around us.

The Doppler Effect dimension of choices conveys how our relationships with other people determine the effects the choices we make individually or collectively as a group. It shows how they impact, change, and create waves in the lives of others.

In the race of life, the Doppler Effect dimension of choice reflects the different effects and change waves the choices we make produce in the lives of those close to us and those who have nothing in common with us.

In the Maze of Choices, our relationships with other people determine the effect the choices we make have on them. These choices can result in grievous or beneficial outcomes. For example, motorists driving on a highway might not necessarily know themselves but the choices they make prior and when they are driving can affect other drivers. When a driver chooses to drive under the influence of alcohol or decides to drive recklessly this might be detrimental to the safety of other motorists, it can result in deadly outcomes.

Doppler Effect dimension of choices reflects or occurs in three dimensions: position, location, and proximity. Therefore, the little or no connection people have with each other, the little or no effect the choices they make will have on others. The position a person occupies in the lives of others will also influence the effects that the choices a person makes will have in the lives of others. Our locations, relationships, and proximities with others determine the impact and effect the choices they make will have or produce in our lives and in the lives of others.

The choices we make can become recurring decimals in our lives that cut across the board.

Droste Effect Dimension—Choices are reflective. The Droste Effect operative dimension of choice reflects how the choices we make in one aspect of life can have a Droste Effect in other areas of our lives.

The choices we make have the power to influence, control, and affect other areas of our lives. The effect and outcomes of the choices we make in one area of our lives can be seen in other areas of our lives. However, the magnitude or degree of the effect of our choices varies. The choices we make in one aspect of our lives has the power to create a recurring impact in other areas of our lives.

In the Maze of Choices, most times we are not aware of the effect and the power inherent in our freedom to make choices. We sometimes take it for granted and make choices flippantly. The reality is that the choices we make in one area of our lives have the power to promote or corrupt other areas in our lives and sometimes in the lives of others.

Any good or bad choice we make in one area of life can interact with other areas of our lives because choices have the power to cut across the board. For example, the choices we make in the area of our health can control and affect other areas of our lives, such as our finances, physical and mental well-being, social life, and relationships.

When we make the choice to be selfish, unfriendly, or self-centered, the impact of such choices, is reflected in our dealings and relationships with others. Likewise, when we make the choice to be kind, grateful, thankful, or appreciative and gracious, it can have a tremendous effect on other aspects of our lives.

Our choices have tentacles that encroach, pull, control, and affect other areas of our lives. The choices we make have the possibility to become recurring decimals that reflect in different areas of our lives, including our financial, social, physical, spiritual, and mental areas of our lives.

Halo Effect Dimension—Our programming from our backgrounds controls and influences our dealings with others. Our ideals, beliefs, opinions, and experiences about someone or something have the power to influence the choices we make concerning the individuals or situations.

The halo effect dimension of choices is in operation in the Maze of Choices when we make choices based on first impressions, past experiences, previous information, performances, or former outcomes.

All these have the tendency to impede our ability to make relevant judgment. The possibility of being biased in any issue of life is determined by our upbringing, pre-knowledge, information, and experiences. The halo effect dimension of choice can have adverse effects on our choices in any realm of life as a result of being biased.

When we make choices based on our past experiences, performances, outcomes, or first impressions, it influences the subsequent choices we will make. The possibility to be biased in evaluating a situation in order to make a rational decision is impeded by our history and past experiences. Our past experiences, results, outcomes, and first impressions can set the wheel of choice in motion in all realms of life.

Therefore, the buoyancy of our results and outcomes has a greater influence and effect on our future choices. When our former choices produce a favorable or significant outcome, it makes it easier for us to make a similar choice in future situations and happenings. In the

OPERATIVE DIMENSIONS OF CHOICE

Maze of Choices, our backgrounds, past experiences, and beliefs have the power to influence the choices we make in all spheres of life.

Instruction Dimension—In the Maze of Choices, instructions represent information given or written, which coincides with commands and directives meant to aid each one of us to make choices that will either help us succeed or fail in an area of life. The choices we make, with the instruction or information we have in the Maze of Choices, will determine the realm in which we will operate in life, because all aspects of life are governed by instructions.

Success or failure in any area of life is rooted in our choices as they relate to instructions given to us. These instructions have the inherent power to impart knowledge, guidance, and detailed directions on how to go about issues in different spheres of life.

Our outcomes and experiences in life are anchored on the instructions we choose to obey or ignore. Every achievement in any spectrum of life is traceable to instructions we obey and apply to situations. For example, in the realm of relationships, there are written and unwritten instructions upholding every relationship. Our ability to recognize and obey the instructions guarding each relationship will determine the solidity and buoyancy of our relationships. This is true because the instruction that governs workplace relationships is different from that governing marriage.

The instruction dimension of choices is very active in creating and determining our experiences and circumstances in life. It also has the power to change situations and circumstances in our lives. In the Maze of Choices, the instruction we chose to obey or ignore is an operative force that determines our outcomes in life. Also, it is crucial to note that not all instructions are beneficial to us. For this reason, it is vital to examine every instruction and see if the instruction carries a legal or illicit command or directive in order to avert making ourselves and others the victims of our choices.

CHOICES ARE FORERUNNERS

Our intention is a major determinant in the choices we make and the trigger that propels all activities in the streets of life.

Intention Dimension—In the Maze of Choices, behind every choice we make there is always an underlying force known as *intention*. Intention is a predominant force that acts as a propeller to engender the choices we make.

In every choice we make, there is always the possibility to make choice intentionally. The intention dimension of choices is a premeditated dimension of choice where we, individually and collectively as a group, consciously and subconsciously, make choices to align with our intentions.

The intentions of our hearts constantly influence the choices we make. There are two sides to this dimension. They are positive intention and negative intention.

- *The positive intention dimension of choice*—In the Maze of Choices, the positive intention dimension of choice is when we as individuals, or collectively as a group, choose to be kind, generous, helpful, and nice to others.

    It is a dimension where we choose to overlook the weakness or shortcomings of others. It is a dimension that refuses the path of being judgmental in dealing with others and their weaknesses. This type of choice is made intentionally and consciously. It is a dimension in the Maze of Choices where we choose to see the good, the possibility, and the strength in others.

    Positive, intentional choices go against segregation, discrimination, and minority versus majority mindsets. They eliminate discrimination and finger-pointing. Intentional dimension of choices are choices targeted to service and selflessness to humanity and are purposeful. It is a dimension where we individually, or collectively as a group, purposefully extend a hand of empathy, kindness, love, solidarity, and friendship to others in spite of who they are or their backgrounds. It is a dimension of choice where we intentionally choose to nurture and not torture others.

- *The negative intention dimension of choice*—This dimension of choice-making is always backed with selfishness and selfish goals. It is a dimension where a person always puts his or herself constantly as a priority above the interests of others. This is done even when the choices made might be harmful and unprofitable to others.

  It is a premediated choice that creates havoc and pain in the lives of others. A lot of people have become victims where an individual or a group of people intentionally set out to frustrate and harm another person via the choices they make. It is an evil act that can be triggered by competition, gossip, ill-will, ignorance, or hatred. Many people have become victims of such negative, intentional choices made by others.

The intention behind every choice we make will eventually climax into outcomes, happenings, and events in our lives and in the lives of others.

Irritation Dimension—Every choice we make always causes a reaction: a reaction that can birth peace, comfort, or anarchy and discomfort. A continuous engagement in making poor or bad choices will only result in irritations.

Poor, bad, or wrong choices trigger irritation in all spheres of life. They result in annoyance, vexation, displeasure, resentment, and discomfort, all of which can be detrimental to us and others. The irritation dimension of choices can be orchestrated by the choices we make personally and by the choices of others. This is the scary part of choice-making, because the choices we or other people make can determine our comfort or discomfort in life. For example, the poor or bad choices of an authority figure in a family or organization can cause irritation in the lives of others by creating unnecessary stress and turmoil. Another example is the chaos, pain, discomfort, sorrow, and anarchy created by bullies in the lives of their victims and families. The irritation dimension of choices occurs when the poor, bad, or wrong choices we and others make become thorns in our flesh and the flesh of others. This can affect a myriad of people and, in the process, determine the course of events in our lives and in the lives of others.

Memories are priceless and timeless. Memories unveil and reveal our past choices.

The Past Dimension—Our past and past choices always have a way of catching up with us to interfere, intervene, influence, command, control, help, and decide our lots in life. Our past choices directly and indirectly determine and control our present well-being. The choices we make today are being laid on the foundation of the choices we made yesterday, which will eventually determine the events that transpire in our tomorrow.

The choices we've made in the past can be good or bad, right or wrong, just or unjust. They all have a way of announcing and inviting themselves into our lives to aid or intercept the activities of today and future. It is crucial for us to realize that whatever situations or circumstances we might be facing today or in the future, they are being triggered by the choices we personally or others made in the past.

The choices we've made in the past determine the events, occurrences, and transactions in our lives. Our past choices create the situations and circumstances we face personally or collectively as a group. Likewise, whatever choices we are making amid our present situations or circumstances will determine our future experiences. In any area of life where there is an element of satisfaction or dissatisfaction, the choices we've made, and others have made on our behalf, in the past are the source of the satisfaction or dissatisfaction we and/or others experience.

OPERATIVE DIMENSIONS OF CHOICE

On the other hand, our past choices act as mirrors and also our memory bank. Our past choices act as mirrors in our lives whereby we can look, check, and see areas where we can make amendments or adjustments when necessary. They serve as our memory bank for reflection because memories are priceless and timeless. When we visit our past to reflect on our past choices, we take trips down memory lane. This dimension helps us to avert making the same bad mistakes again and, in turn, helps us make better situations in our present.

Ignoring our past choices and not learning from them is like denying the existence of our shadows and we wind up making the same mistakes again. However, this dimension is not an excuse for us to bury our heads in the past. It is an opportunity to retrospectively reflect on the choices we've made in the past in order to learn and help us to make better choices in the future.

Finally, the choices we've made in the past should be seen as mirrors to reflect, learn, unlearn or re-learn, correct, check, and balance the equations in our lives and to clean and refresh ourselves, to have a personal self-talk, to forgive ourselves and others and to create conducive atmospheres, where we can make choices that will avert any distress or discomfort in our future.

The past doesn't necessarily have to be an obstacle in our lives when we choose to learn from our past mistakes and let them go. We do not stay or stand the whole day or year in front of a mirror, instead we stand in front of a mirror for a moment to check, adjust, correct, or put finishing touches to our dressing and before moving on. Reflecting on our past choices for a moment will help us to make amendments, adjustments, and corrections, to areas of our lives where we need to improve ourselves in order for us to avoid making the same mistake again or having history repeat itself negatively.

Planning Dimension—In the Maze of Choices, there is no endeavor in life that can become successful without planning. We plan by choice. It is a dimension in the Maze of Choices that is vital to every aspect of life. For any goal or dream to become a reality, there has to be a detailed method, that includes structured steps and a procedure that must be taken to make our dreams a reality.

Planning is an operative dimension in the Maze of Choices that enhances our successes in any good endeavor of life. The planning dimension of choice is time oriented. It is aimed at a targeted result or goal.

In the Maze of Choices, the place of planning is the junction of investment and preparation for future success and progress. Planning and preparation have the power to change and turn the course of event in the Maze of Choices.

Our desired success in any area of life is a mere wish without planning. Opportunities in life can only yield good results when we choose to plan ahead of time. All success in different spheres of life begins with planning,

Setting right priorities enhances our ability to make good choices.

Priority Dimension—In life, our priorities orchestrate our choices. Our choices in life's affairs are mostly anchored on our priorities. Our choices reflect our priorities in every aspect of life. Our priorities have the power to influence the choices we make regarding our relationships, social, spiritual, mental lives, and even in our finances.

In the Maze of Choices, we make choices based on the scale of preference and our priorities. Our priorities are vital organizers and contractors in constructing our paths in the Maze of Choices. In the streets of life, all the choices we make are triggers that enforce all of our activities in all spheres of life while the choices we make are organized and mobilized by our priorities. In all areas of life, whatever we deem as sources of concern in our lives are what catches our attention, which eventually becomes uppermost in our hierarchies of precedence.

OPERATIVE DIMENSIONS OF CHOICE

It is very important to set our priorities right because they affect and influence the choices we make. Our choices are witnesses in our lives that can testify for us or against us. Priority dimension of choices reflects our interests, desires, and concerns. Setting our priorities right engenders progress and stability in the areas of life where we make the choice to prioritize our time, relationships, programs, goals, and desires.

In the race of life, every action reflects the choices we make because our choices are activated by action to align with our preferences or priorities. In terms of relationships, the behavior and response of people to us individually or collectively as a group shows our position and the place we hold in their lives. Every relationship has an invisible scale that measures the relational capital in terms of the choices we make regarding the relationship. The priority operative dimension of choices shows our preferences, interests, concerns, and the position we place the people in our lives and vice versa. In all of our dealings as human beings, whatever we deem as a priority will act as boosters that orchestrate the choices we make and actions we take, which will eventually translate into activities and transactions in the streets of life.

Procrastination is the umbilical cord that fuels failure, stagnation, and retrogression in people's lives.

Procrastination Dimension—Procrastination is the refusal to take action at the appropriate time. We procrastinate both in conducive and un-conducive conditions of life. Procrastination is abortive in nature and it is an operative dimension in the Maze of Choice that results in futility in those areas of life where we choose to procrastinate. Procrastination is a major tool which we use unknowingly to place barriers on our progress and advancement in life. *Procrastination is simply a choice made to continuously shift the goalpost of success in our lives.* In the race of life, procrastination is a time waster; however, not all men are victims of procrastination.

Procrastination is an undeniable dimension in the Maze of Choices because it can become a weapon of offence in the area of life where we have chosen to use it as a weapon against ourselves. Procrastination is very subtle, if not unmasked in time. It can rob us of our crown and fame in life. Procrastination is the umbilical cord that fuels failure, stagnation, and retrogression in people's lives.

Profit Dimension—Most times, people see the word "profit" as a financial term, but profit covers a broader spectrum than finance. Our understanding and perception of the word profit determine the choices we will make in various situations and happenings of life. Once we have an in-depth understanding of the word profit, the choices we will make per situation will be different.

The choices we make in life determine the profit we will make in all our various endeavors. Our profitability in different areas of life is based on the choices we make. Our choices have an inherent power to set a wheel in motion in the direction that might be beneficial or detrimental to us and others. Every good, just, and right choice we make has the power to produce profit in our lives and in the lives of others.

Living a life of peace and stability based on the choices we make is a profit to us and those who loves us. The choices we make in every area of our lives have the power to bring us profit or losses because they determine what we attract into our lives. Every time we make choices in different areas of our lives, we are either engaging in addition and multiplication, which eventually brings us profit, or subtraction and division, which bring losses.

Question-and-Answer Dimension—Generally, questions broaden our knowledge and influence the choices we make. Some questions attract answers; often, the questions we ask ourselves and others around us determine the answers we get.

The questions we ask and the answers we get in return have the power to influence the choices we make in different situations of life.

OPERATIVE DIMENSIONS OF CHOICE

This question-and-answer dimension of choices has the power to direct and redirect our steps in life.

In the race of life, the questions we are willing to ask ourselves and the answers we get, in terms of feedback, can orchestrate the choices we make regarding any situation. In the streets of life, questions and answers can be denominators in all transactions that transpire in various spheres or endeavors. Questions and the answers are pointers to choices most likely to be made in any situation. The questions asked and the answers received have the power to control, influence, and determine the choices we make. We engage in the question-and-answer dimension of choices every day whether we realize it or not. These questions can be internal questions we ask ourselves personally or external questions we ask other people, and the veracity or mendacity of the answers received influences the choices we make.

Ripple Effect Dimension—Every choice we make at different aspects of life has the power to create a ripple effect in the areas where we least expected. The ripple effect dimension of choices can cause a series of events to occur in various areas of our lives. The ripple effect dimension of choices can have a positive or negative effect, which might eventually create changes that can be temporary or long-lasting.

One good choice can trigger a series of other choices that are profitable to us and others. Likewise, one wrong or bad choice can engender a series of events that can cause pain, heartache, and sorrow in the lives of other people. Sometimes, these might trigger a need for a reform that might be beneficial to generations to come.

In the Maze of Choices, a single choice, whether good or bad, right or wrong, can have a ripple effect, which can spread and affect or benefit more people in a larger scale than we can imagine or think possible.

The ripple effect dimensions of the choices made by a person or group of people in the past have become a generational blessing or a problem in the world today. The choices we make individually or collectively as a group today can result in triggering ripple effects that will affect or bless the future generations.

In the Maze of Choices, good choices made by a parent, a teacher, student, an executive, a government, a leader, a pilot, a doctor, or a scientist can trigger ripple effects that will be beneficial to humanity. Even in things that might seems trivial, just one choice can cause a series of events that can make a difference in the lives of people and in our world.

Sinkhole Dimension—Sometimes in life, we make choices that can create a vacuum in our lives and in the lives of others. These choices can create a sinkhole. Most times, the end results of the choices we make cannot be predicted and the collateral damage cannot be pre-evaluated.

In the Maze of Choices, some choices might seem right at the moment of making the choice, but the end result can become a sinkhole. The sinkhole dimension of our choices occurs when our choices create destructive eruptions in our lives and in the lives of others.

When we individually or collectively as a group engage in making bad, poor, wrong, and illicit choices on a continuous basis, it causes an erosion, an erosion that gradually diminishes and destroys different spheres of our lives to create a hole or vacuum that is unfillable. This vacuum can lead to a sudden collapse in an area of our lives where poor, bad, or ill choices have been made.

In the nutshell, the sinkhole dimension of choices occurs when we, as humans, continuously make destructive choices that drains, diminishes, and downgrades our potentials, opportunities, and possibilities in life. Once we create sinkholes in our lives by the choices we make, whenever a boisterous, blustery wind of life blows, it causes a collapse in the areas of life where the choice has been made. Below are some areas of life where we as humans, knowingly and unknowingly, create sinkholes in our lives and sometimes in the lives of others:

- Emotional sinkhole
- Financial sinkhole
- Health sinkhole
- Relationships sinkhole
- Social sinkhole
- Spiritual sinkhole
- Trust sinkhole

Every challenge comes to build, develop, or destroy our character. Whatever side we might end in the character gauge is determined by the choices we make amid the challenges and situations of life.

Situation Dimension—In the Maze of Choices, we create some situations and circumstances in our lives by the choices we make, and we can change certain situations or circumstances in our lives by the choices we make. Some situations, issues, challenges, and circumstances are created by the choices we make personally or collectively as a group.

Situations or challenges are bound to confront each one of us at one point or another in life. However, our reactions, in terms of the choices we make prior to and in times of challenges will determine the outcome. Challenges and situations of life most times create an opportunity for us as human beings to exercise our power and freedom to choose. Whatever we choose creates the atmospheric conditions and situations in our lives. These issues or situations raise their heads at different phases in life and our reception via the choices we make will determine the outcomes.

Multiple options, distractions, hurdles, challenges, situations, and events are some of the constant occupants we encounter in the Maze of Choices. They all influence the choices we make to create situations and experiences in our lives. As we journey through various paths in life, situations, happenings, and events are frequent flyers that are always present with us. The choices we make amid these situations or events that transpires in our lives will determine our outcomes in all realms of life.

In all spheres in life, situations and circumstances keep changing to align with the choices we make. To some extent, we create the situations and transactions that transpire in our lives by the choices we make personally and by those that others make on our behalf.

Soul Dimension—The soul dimension is crucial because our souls have a way of influencing and propelling our choices. Our souls have three parts that directly and indirectly influence all the choices we make in every aspect of life. The three parts in the soul are as follows:

- Emotion
- Mind
- Will

These three parts that comprise the soul play pivotal rules in influencing the choices we make, and they eventually determine our experiences and outcomes in life.

In the Maze of Choices, we need to discipline our emotions in order to make good choices.

Emotion—In the Maze of Choices, our emotional state has the power to determine our outcomes and experiences in life and also in the lives of others, especially when we allow our emotions to be in charge of us instead of us being in control of our emotions.

Our emotions have ways of interrupting our abilities to make rational choices. Emotions can be positive or negative or neutral. Our emotions can become obstacles that hinder our abilities to make good choices. It is crucial to deal with our emotions by putting them in check before making choices because what we feel is indirectly transmitted into the choices we make.

OPERATIVE DIMENSIONS OF CHOICE

When we continually engage our emotions in our choices, our emotions become a dominating factor that controls the choices we make. It is crucial to balance our emotions in the emotional scale so as not to be on the extreme side of the scale. The readings on our emotional scale of life will affect and determine the choices we make in every situation.

On the emotional scale, love and hate are common denominators that trigger other emotions in the Maze of Choices. Emotions can be beneficial or destructive. Emotional eruption, especially in the negative such as hate, anger, and bitterness can be destructive, while positive emotions, such as love, compassion, and kindness are good but can still result in unacceptable compromise and being unfair in making the right choices. They can also make us victims when they are not well-balanced on the emotion scale.

Any choice we make under the influence of our emotions, especially the negative emotions, can result in irrational judgment. In the Maze of Choices, our emotions can place an embargo on our power to choose, which eventually impedes our abilities to choose rightly.

Both negative, positive, and neutral emotions have ways of obstructing, propelling, and influencing the choices we make. Balancing our emotions in the emotion scale is vital in order to avoid making irrational choices.

The Mind—The mind of human beings is the drawing board where all transactions of life are being drawn and mapped out. There is no limitation to what the mind can fathom. It has the power to stretch or shrink. Our victory and defeat in any realm of life begins in the mind. When we are victorious in our minds, it reflects in our choices. When we win the battles in our minds, nothing can conquer us because most transactions in our lives transmit from our minds.

> **When you have not been conquered in your mind, nothing can conquer you.**
> **—Edo Proverb**

CHOICES ARE FORERUNNERS

Every good and evil happening begins from the mind. The mind transmits all the thoughts, choices, and actions of all human dealings. Whatever transpires in our minds is seen in the choices we make because the mind is the source of all transactions that take place in the streets of life. Nothing takes place without first being processed and transmitted from the mind.

Our mental capacity influences the choices we make in all spheres of life. The imaginations of our minds cannot be separated from the choices we make. When the imaginations in our minds are evil or good, the choices we make align with our state of mind.

No transaction takes place in the streets of life without being first executed in the mind. Our minds are the control towers of the choices we make. Our state of mind influences the choices we make. A victorious mindset makes choices that propagate victory, while a victim mindset makes choices that enforce victim-oriented outcomes, and a gossip mindset fuels division and disunity.

The force of our will is a strong determinant in the Maze of Choices. It is an ever- present force that influences our choices.

The Will—The force of our will is a strong determinant in the Maze of Choices, and it is an ever -present force in all the choices we make in all realms of life. It is crucial to know that in all realms of life, our will is not constant because we can be strong-willed in one area of life and less willed, in another area of life. That is why we sometimes make poor choices in one area of life and better choices in another area. The choices we make reflect the strength of our will in different realms of life.

Our *will*, which is free, can be engaged freely in all realms of life. That is why it is called free will, and this *free* will has been given to every human being as a mechanism by which we can make choices in all spheres of life.

OPERATIVE DIMENSIONS OF CHOICE

In the Maze of Choices, our *will* is an operative dimension that influences our choices in all areas of life. Anytime we make choices, our free will is being tested. At that point in time, our free will can become a source of protection or destruction, depending on how we exercise our free will. In the Maze of Choices, our free will is a dimension that is in operation in all the choices we make. Whatever we choose to do with our free will becomes our choice, irrespective of the external factors or influences that might act as catalysts to facilitate the choices we make in different spheres of life. At the end, it is our *will* that influences our choices. The choices we make are anchored in our will; that is why our will is a propeller for our choices. Our willpower is our power to choose. Whatever transpires in our will influences the choices we make because the free will of every human being is actively involved in the choices we make, whether we are aware of it or not.

Our will is a major determinant of the choices we make, because our choices conform with our will. Just as we cannot separate ourselves from the choices we make, we cannot separate our will from the choices we make.

Whether we are aware of it or not, every choice we make aligns with our free will (willpower). In the Maze of Choices, our will reflects and showcases the strength of our willpower. However, our willpower might be stronger in one area than another, which is why we can be more rational and productive in making good choices in one area of life yet make terrible, poor choices in another area of life. Our will can be

- *Strong Will*
- *Weak Will*

How we engage our free will determines our destines and how we sail through life.

Strong Will—In any area of life where we are fully engaging our willpower in making good, just, and/or right choices, it shows we have developed our will to be strong in that area of life.

Weak Will—When we make choices that engage our willpower negatively or by complying with the will of others to make bad, poor, or illicit choices, it confirms that our willpower is weak.

Finally, any time we engage in making choices, we are directly exercising our *free will* in spite of the external or internal influences. Therefore, at the Maze of Choices, we, (you and I) are the dominators who have the power to decide what to do with *our* willpower.

You = Your Free Will = Your Choices

The choices we make in different areas of our lives act as thermometers that measure our success and as thermostats that regulate and maintain the vibrancy of our successes.

Thermometer and Thermostat Dimension—In the Maze of Choices, the choices we make in different areas of our lives place a bar over our lives. This eventually regulates our attainments in life and controls the in-flow of different traffic in our lives.

The choices we make act as thermometers and measuring gauges that measure our performances, which determine our results in life. How far we soar and shoot in life are anchored to the choices we make in various endeavors of life.

At different junctions in life, the choices we make in different affairs of our lives become key performance indicators that measure our performances and determine the gratification we receive or ramification we earn.

The choices we make in different affairs of our lives also act as our thermostats that automatically regulate all conditions in our lives, just as the thermostat has the ability to establish and maintain a desired temperature. Also, in life, the choices we make act as thermostats that create, regulate, maintain, and establish the atmospheric, mental, social, financial, physiological, and emotional conditions in our lives.

The choices we make have the inherent power to initiate change in any area of our lives where we desire a change. All transactions in our lives are controlled by the choices we've made in the past. These choices are the thermometers and thermostats in our lives that control and regulate the various conditions in and around our lives, including, families, communities, and organizations we are part of.

By choice, we can control our thoughts by continuously deleting negative thoughts and harmful information from our minds. We can then upgrade our minds with relevant information that will enhance our lives.

Thought Dimension—Our thinking patterns have tremendous impacts on the choices we make in different areas of life. In the Maze of Choices, our thoughts are vital propellers for the choices we make.

This is true because corrupt, negative, evil, and illicit thinking or thought will result in making evil, negative, and corrupt choices; whereas, positive, good, rich, uplifting, empowering, kind, right, and gracious thinking will result in making choices that are good.

In the Maze of Choices, our environments and events in our lives have ways of infiltrating and controlling our thinking, which eventually affects the choices we make.

Our ability to engage our power of thought positively will enhance our abilities to choose rightly. Just as we cannot separate ourselves from our thoughts, neither can we separate the choices we make from our thoughts. Our choices in all aspects of life are reflections of our thoughts because, as a man thinks, so he is. Our thought patterns affect our perspectives and perceptions, which indirectly or directly influence our choices.

CHOICES ARE FORERUNNERS

The way we think plays a major role in the choices we make. Our minds are the control towers of our thoughts. Every transaction that takes place in our minds and around us has the power to control the choices we make. Whatever accesses our minds through the channels of our eyes and ears can control and determine our thoughts, which eventually affects the choices we make. Whatever transpires in our minds constructs and controls what we think.

That is why it is crucial to continuously delete negative thoughts and harmful information from our minds. While in the process of this, it is upgrading our minds with relevant information that will empower and enhance our thoughts. This is crucial because the transactions in our thinking control our choices.

The more value we place on any aspect of our lives acts as an enhancer in making that area of our lives more productive and colorful.

Value Dimension—Life is a race, and the race of life is run by the choices we make. The value dimension of choices is strongly active in the race of life. The standards we set for ourselves, individually or collectively, control the choices we make in different aspects of our lives.

As humans, we place value on different aspects of our lives, such as material, physical, spiritual, mental, relational, financial, and social. Every day we make choices in all these areas of life to either enhance or mar our value.

The Maze of Choices can become a place where we add value to our lives and the lives of others or diminish our value and that of others. The value we place on different aspect of our lives influence the choices we make. Our choices eventually determine how we act, react, or respond to different activities or happenings that transpire in our lives. The value we place on our relationships, careers, finances, or spiritual and/or general well-being are seen in our actions and dealings. The value we place on each aspect of our lives determines the choices we and others make concerning us.

OPERATIVE DIMENSIONS OF CHOICE

That is why we must consciously and intentionally value ourselves and the blessings of God in our lives, because the value we place on ourselves is seen by others around us. The value we place on ourselves has the power to engender the choices others make about us. We must intentionally make the choice to place value on ourselves, our relationships, and other aspects of our lives, because value is reciprocal in nature. The value we place on different aspects of our lives by the choices we make reflects on us.

Weapon Dimension—Our choices are weapons in our hands that we use to fight both seen and unseen battles of life. Choices can also be an instrument in our hands to harmonize our lives in any area we choose to deploy our power of choice positively. On the other hand, the choices we make can also be a weapon we unknowingly use to create chaos in our lives and in the lives of others.

In life's journey, when we face adverse or difficult situations, our choices become our weapon which we use to conquer or be conquered. The outcome of any challenge or confronting situation of life is at the mercy of the choices we make.

We must intentionally and carefully make choices, because every choice has the power to become a weapon of war or an instrument of peace in our hands. Of course, there are times we all make poor or wrong choices, but the ability to realize that the choices we made were wrong and our ability to make an amendment where necessary will make a world of difference. The choices we make are our weapons and instruments of change in the face of adversity, difficult situations, or favorable situations of life.

Our choices can become instruments of peace, protection, harmony unity or cruelty, violence, anarchy, chaos, and disorder. It all depends on the intentions of our hearts that our choices entail.

Words Dimension—As humans, words are one of our essential modes of communication. Words are an active operative dimension in the Maze of Choices, which we use to communicate and express the choices we make, internally or externally.

We communicate our ideals, thoughts, and feelings through words. Our words are our blueprints that create images and pictures in our minds and in the minds of others. They can be uplifting, encouraging, and empowering or belittling, downgrading, and ridiculing.

We set the course of our lives in motion by our words and sometimes the lives of other who choose to believe or receive our words.

The impact of our words in our lives and the lives of others can have long-lasting positive or negative effects. It depends on what the words entail and the interpretation of the words by the receiver. The operative dimension of words in the affairs of humans is a powerful one because words are not retrievable, once they have been dispatched through spoken or written form.

Just as we cannot undo or retrieve yesterday, the words that have been released in spoken or written form can't be called back. Every derogatory chosen word that has been dispatched cannot be called back once it has been released. Even when we apologize, the damage has been done.

Words are crucial in the Maze of Choices because words have the power to influence and control our choices and actions. Words are the forerunners of all actions and reactions in the streets of life. We set the course of our lives and actions in motion by our words, and sometimes we affect the lives of others who choose to believe, receive, act, react, or respond to our words.

In the mouths and hands of every human being, words are powerful weapons, instruments, and tools, which we use to satisfy our various desires in all realms of life. Our words are weapons we use to pacify, encourage, uplift, educate, influence, control, manipulate, and tarnish ourselves and others.

OPERATIVE DIMENSIONS OF CHOICE

In the streets of life, words have the power to bring peace or start war. They can become weapons in our hands and mouths to hurt, harm, belittle, or destroy ourselves unconsciously or destroy others' self-esteem or self-confidence. One word, whether spoken or written, can have refreshing, empowering, grievous, or devastating effects in the lives of those the words were spoken or written to.

The truth is our words can create miracles or anarchy in our lives and the lives of others. Our words can have negative or positive impacts because words carry substances that are transmittable, which eventually have the ability to control any environment or atmosphere.

Each and every one of us can love or hurt people with our words. Every time we speak or write something to others, we are either touching people's lives positively or negatively with our words. In the Maze of Choices, word dimension of choices is one area of life we must be careful and sensitive to by choosing our words carefully, because our words or word can become a weapon in our mouths and hands to destroy or protect those around us.

Our words, whether written or spoken, are by choice and they are our legacy in the hearts of those they were addressed to.

The words we speak or write can be used as a tool or weapon to

- Accuse
- Boost
- Command
- Condemn
- Edify
- Frighten
- Frustrate
- Groom

CHOICES ARE FORERUNNERS

- Guide
- Infuriate
- Intimidate
- Judge
- Nurture
- Persuade
- Provoke
- Reprove

Finally, in the Maze of Choices, our words are weapons and tools in our hands and mouths, which we use to create inclusiveness or divisiveness in the streets of life. Our words reflect the choices we have made in different affairs of life. Our words whether written or spoken leave a legacy in our hearts and in the hearts of those we address.

> *There is always a gap between our dreams and reality. The only thing that can fill or bridge that gap is the choices we make daily.*

CHAPTER 12

CHOICES GOVERN ALL

EVERY ADVENTURE, VICTORY, success, or failure in life begins with the choices we make. Choices are the fuel, catalyst, booster, energy, and the dominant factor in the equations of life. All activities and transactions in all walks of life are governed by our choices. Our success and achievements in all spheres of life are anchored to the choices we make daily. The choices we make are crucial in balancing the equations of life at different phases in life's journey.

> *Every activity in every walk of life is governed by the choices we make.*

The choices we make are the force that governs our actions, reactions, and outcomes because all aspect of our lives is governed by the power of choice. Unfortunately, not all of us are aware of this reality, that the choices we make are making us and mapping out our lives and destinies.

Our choices act as triggers that initiate all the events and transactions that happen in our lives. The choices we make in different areas of our lives are the vanguards and forerunners of the events and happenings that transpire in our lives. Our choices determine where we are today and where we will be tomorrow.

The veracity of choices is that the choices we make and that others make on our behalf cannot be separated from the events and happenings that transpire in our lives. Just as we cannot separate ourselves from our shadows, we cannot separate ourselves from the realities the choices we make create in our lives.

Our results and outcomes in life are anchored to the choices we make, and choices are integral in balancing the equations of life. Every success or setback in life is directly or indirectly proportional to the choices we've made in the past. The irony is that sometimes the choices of others can also lead to the downfall or success of another person. That is how intrinsic our choices are in governing our lives.

Making choices is a universal and integral part of our existence as humans.

Making Choices Is Part of Our Existence—Choices are vital to our existence and sustenance of human lives. All transactions and actions in the affairs of life are governed by our choices. There is no transaction in the streets of life that is not triggered by the choices we make, individually or collectively.

In every area of life, our history reflects the choices we made, and the choices others made on our behalf. Likewise, our future is mapped and guided by the choices we are making right now and the ones we will make in the future.

Making choices is crucial to us as the air we breathe, because we cannot live without making choices. Even in situations or circumstances where things seem impossible, directly or indirectly, we are still engaging our power of choice. In all spheres of life, we are always presented with options to choose between life or death, good or evil, right or wrong, guide or derail, build or destroy, bind or loose, love or hate. Every day, we engage and deploy our power of choice in one area or another. Making choices is a universal and integral part of our existence as humans.

In any situation and happening in our lives, whatever we choose is our choice.

Choices Are Vital and Integral—There are times in life where we have no power to make some choices. For example, we cannot choose our family, or country we were born into, or our race, genetic makeup, and language. Once we are born, the power to choose becomes eminent in our lives as we journey through life.

Whether we are using our power of choice positively or negatively, wisely or unwisely, it is a choice we make knowingly and unknowingly. How we utilize our power of choice in our lives will determine how smooth, successful, or stressful our life's journey will be. We will live by the choices we make. The choices we make in the affairs of life are what determine the buoyancies of the transactions that take place in our lives.

Every transaction and event that transpires in our lives is anchored to the choices we make in different aspects of life. Therefore, making choices are vital and integral in the affairs of life. Choices govern all areas of our lives. They are an integral force that determines our successes and progress in life. Making choices is an integral part in our existence because the choices we make in one area of our lives can have across-the-board effects in other areas of our lives.

Making choices is vital and integral in our lives because no one can live without making choices, neither can we separate our results, performances, or outcomes in life from the choices we make. Ultimately, how beautiful, colorful, and awesome any area of our lives is stems from the choices we make.

Our results, outcomes, and experiences in life are the products that come out of the mine of our choices.

CHOICES ARE FORERUNNERS

Our Choices and Results Are Inseparable—Every result or outcome in life is directly or indirectly proportional to the choices we make personally, or others make on our behalf. The results we produce in our lives cannot be separated from the choices we've made or refused to make.

Choices are like seeds that a farmer sows, just one good choice can yield a tremendous rich harvest of positivity. In any area of life where we might not be contented, our choices amid the issues of concern in our lives have the power to change our results and outcomes.

Whenever we want to have good results in life, we must endeavor to make choices that will ensure the desired result is achieved. The choices we make, and others make affect and influence our results in life.

Choices Can Be Indelible—Making choices might be common to all human beings, but it is an error to think that the choices we make in different areas of our lives just disappear or evaporate into air. Our choices don't disappear or evaporate. Rather they act as forerunners that go into our futures to pave the way and prepare a reception for us and others. They eventually control the events and happenings that take place in our futures, and sometimes generations after us.

In the streets of life, every transaction and activity of every human being is sponsored by the choices made in the past and in the present. The choices we and others made in the past are the pathfinders and precursors for the choices that are being made now and in the future. Every choice we make lays a foundation and creates room for us to make more choices. Even the choices we make flippantly or ignorantly can become recurring decimals in our lives.

Every result we get in life is determined by the choices we make. These choices become springboards and launch pads for success or setback in the area of life where the choices were made. Since we cannot fully predict or envisage the outcome of the choices we are making, it crucial for us to engage our power of choice positively in order to impact our lives and the lives of others for the benefit of humanity. Therefore, impacting our lives and the lives of others begins with making choices with good intentions in all areas of life for the general interest of all humans, because choices made are indelible. One choice made can create a generational blessing or a problem.

Choices Are a Threshold—There is no aspect of life where each and every one of us are not confronted to choose or make choices. Daily, from the rising to the setting of the sun, we all engage in one form of choice-making or another. The choices we make in different areas of life can have beneficial or adverse effects on us and others in our domain.

The choices we make can become sources of collateral blessings or create collateral damage. They can become avenues to create a generation's solution or problem. The choices made in the past by our predecessors are major sponsors of the transactions transpiring in different spectrums of our society and world today, and the choices we are making today in our various endeavors and positions will determine the transactions that will confront or comfort future generations. The choices we are making right now in our various official or unofficial capacities and the positions we are occupying, individually or collective as a group, are our gifts or problems to the next generations.

> *Our choices can become collateral blessings or create collateral damage.*

Collateral Blessing—There is a saying in Edo language, "*There is something in a seed.*" A seed can become a tree that produces a truckload of harvest of good or bad fruits. Our choices are embedded with potential to become blessings, or curses; it all depends on what our choices entail. Every good or just choice we make in different areas of life will result in a harvest with a beneficial outcome. The good and just choices we make individually or collectively as a group can become generational blessings where children unborn become beneficiaries of the good choices made by their predecessors.

CHOICES ARE FORERUNNERS

In all spheres of life, the good and right choices we make individually or as a group can create a positive impact in the lives of a family, a community, an organization, a country, a continent, and in the world.

Today, all around the world, there are choices made by the predecessors of different countries that have become generational blessings to their citizens. On a family level, there are choices made by the patriarch and matriarch in some families that have transcended to become generational blessings to their present generations. It is vital to know that the choices we make in different areas of our lives have successors, which are called generational blessings or collateral damage.

Collateral Damage—The choices we make are not limited in nature but are multidimensional, because the choices we make have the power to influence, affect, and control multiple aspects of our lives.

That is why the choices we make in one area of our lives have the power to determine our outcomes, results, and experiences in other areas of our lives, and sometimes in the lives of other people known or unknown to us. The choices we make personally and that others make on our behalf have the power to interfere, control, and determine the affairs of our lives and the lives of others.

For example, the collateral damage of the choice a person made to go drinking in a pub and became drunk, which resulted in a ghastly accident that claimed the life of another person, is irrecoverable. Or consider a careless shooter's choice to shoot that claimed the lives of others leaves a vacuum in the lives of the victims' families that cannot be filled. Choices have consequences.

The choices we make, and others make in different areas of life can have unilateral, bilateral, or multilateral impacts in our lives and in the lives of others, because choices have the power to cut across the board. Most times, bad, poor, or wrong choices result in collateral damage that can affect generations to come. With this vividly engraved in our minds, it is crucial to know that the freedom to choose is a freedom embedded with responsibility for ourselves and others.

This freedom should not be taken for granted, because the bad or ill choices we make in different affairs of life can result in collateral damage. The collateral damage of our choices might not be reversible, especially when the person making the choices is in a position to lead and govern others. The choices a person or people in the realm of authority makes on behalf of others can create generational problems where unborn children will pay the price for the poor, bad, or selfish choices made by a leader or an influencer. It is crucial for each and every one of us to reflect on our history in order to avoid making choices that will create a generational problem for the next generations or endanger or mortgage our freedom and the freedom of generations to come.

As a parent, leader, or a fellow human being, our choices have the power to outlive us to become generational blessings or problems for those who come after us.

Choices Can Create Generational Solutions or Problems— Sometimes in life some of us are not aware of the fact that the freedom to choose is a freedom embedded with responsibility, that our choices individually or collectively as a group have the inherent power to create a generational solution or problem. In all realms of life, our freedom to choose has the power to become a place of bondage and an avenue of creating problems for ourselves and others that might affect many generations.

Today, we enjoy the comfort from technology such as cheaper ways of communicating through the various apps, online learning to enrich our knowledge bank, easy access to information, and technology that advances medical knowledge that leads to healthier living. All these have made life comfortable but on the flip side, the choices some of us are making regarding our advancement in technology have become a source of concern that might create generational problems.

CHOICES ARE FORERUNNERS

The choices we make can create generational solutions or generational problems.

The possibility to create a generational solution or problem is embedded in the choices we make in all realms of life. Creating a generational solution or problem begins with just one choice. One good choice can make a difference in the lives of people, and one bad choice can set a destructive wheel in motion in the lives of people. The destinies of future generations are determined and governed by the choices we make today.

> *We must be mindful of the choices we make because our choices will dictate and influence how we live our lives and, to some degree, the lives of others.*

CHAPTER 13

BE MINDFUL

Sadly, we will not only live by the choices we make individually but sometimes we might have to live by the poor and ill choices of others. That is the fact and the reality someone is living right now. Please be mindful of the choices you are making.

IN LIFE'S JOURNEY, we travel through different paths and phases in life based on the choices we make, and others make on our behalf. The choices we make at each phase of our lives determine how smooth or rough, safe or dangerous, our journey will be. Therefore, it is crucial to be careful and mindful of the choices we make, because choices are not defunct but extant in nature.

While all choices in the Maze of Choices might seem right, not all choices are right or good. Our secret and open choices have the power to determine our courses in life. The secret choices we make that we might think nobody else is aware of always have a way to catch up with us to give their verdict, a verdict that might be for us or against.

CHOICES ARE FORERUNNERS

It is vital to be mindful of the choices we make, whether secretly or openly, in order not to endanger our lives and the lives of others known and unknown to us. Being mindful of the choices we make secretly is crucial, because life always has a way of throwing light on our choices, including the poor, bad, and ill choices we've made. The secret choices we make, especially the bad and ill choices, will always make us and those close to us the victims of their consequences.

At every point in life, we are presented with options that are both good and bad. However, we must be mindful of the choices we make, even if we have been given the freedom to make choices. This is quite daunting because the freedom to choose is a freedom embedded with responsibility, which will determine our outcomes and experiences in life and a freedom embedded with responsibility that will influence the experiences and fate of other people. This freedom is wrapped with responsibility that will orchestrate the events that transpire in our lives and the lives of others.

Whatever choice we make and act upon automatically eliminates all other options available once the choice wheel has been set in motion, so we must be mindful of the choices we make.

We must be mindful of our choices, because choices govern all aspects of life and not all choices are revocable once they have been made. No matter how small or insignificant we might think a choice might be, it still has the power to hurt us and others. Therefore, no matter how small the bad or ill choices we make might be, they have the power to create havoc and pains in our lives and the lives of those dear to us.

As small as mosquitoes might be, mosquitoes have the ability to have a deadly impact in the lives of those they have infested with malaria parasites. Likewise, all those seemingly small, poor, illicit, and secret choices we make have the power to hurt and harm others in our lives, which is why we need to be mindful our choices.

It is vital to always be conscious of the fact that the choices we make can carry rewards or retributions, and our choices are transactions in our lives that will embrace us and make us because the choices we make affect our lives on all fronts.

We make choices and the choices we make will eventually embrace us and make us.

Choices Affect All Fronts—In the race of life, the choices we make in one area of life have the power to control and determine what transpire in other areas of our lives. Hence, the choices we make affect all fronts including our:

- Career development
- Educational development
- Financial life
- Health life
- Relationship
- Social life
- Spiritual life

Every day, as we engage in our various assignments and fulfill our purposes on earth, the choices we make are either aligning us or derailing us from our purposes.

Our choice are major determinants that propel us to fulfill our purposes on earth. Therefore, it is crucial to make good choices because it is in our power to do so irrespective of the prevailing circumstances in order to avoid being the victims of our own choices.

No one can exist without making choices and neither can we separate our lives from the choices we make. The activities that transpire in our lives are being controlled and sustained by our choices. Therefore, all aspects of our lives are being orchestrated and propelled by our choices. Some of our choices are revocable while some are irrevocable.

We cannot undo yesterday; likewise, some of our choices cannot be undone, especially when the life of another person has been marred, affected, or destroyed due to the choices we've made in the past.

Some bad choices are revocable, while some are totally irrevocable. Sorrow and regrets cannot revoke a choice that has cost another person his or her life.

Choices Are Either Revocable or Irrevocable—Today, we live in a world where personal gain and comfort are paramount in the minds of many people. People engage in making different kind of choices; irrespective of the havoc or pain their choices create in the lives of their fellow human beings.

Some of these choices might be revocable while some are totally irrevocable. Any choice that tampers with the life and welfare of another person is a bad choice, and the damage or havoc it can create in the life of the person might be irrevocable. Sorrow and regrets cannot revoke a choice that may have cost another person his or her life, neither will it lessen the pain of those who have been hurt or harmed by the careless choices made by others.

Not all mistakes can be remedied. We have to be mindful of our choices.

It is very important to ensure that our consciences are void of things that might pose threats or harm to the lives of others while making choices. Any choice that will derail or lead others astray is a choice that is harmful.

In our various dealings, whether trivial or profound, it is mandatory that we do not sow bad seeds that we are not willing to reap in our own lives in the lives of others. Any person who will not want to mourn the death of his or her loved ones should not make the choices that will threaten the lives of others.

It is crucial not to take the freedom to make choices for granted, because any choice that make others fall or that puts others in harm's way is irrevocable once the damage has been done. We must be mindful of the choices we are making, because the open and secret choices we make are embedded with implications and benefits.

> **The pleasures of bad, evil, and illicit choices last for a moment; but their repercussions and retributions last for a lifetime.**

Implications and Benefits of Our Choices—Our choices can affect or empower our lives and the lives of others directly or indirectly. There are implications attached to the choices we make. That is why every experience, reward, retribution, and outcome in life are collections and summaries of the choices we've made and acted on. In all spheres of life, we must be mindful of the choices we make because they have the ability to act in the following ways in our lives and in the lives of others:

- A Stimulus
- An Inhibitor
- A Magnet
- A Taskmaster
- A Pathfinder
- A Repellant

> **Our choices act as stimuli that incite various changes that occur in our lives and in the lives of others.**

Our Choices are Stimuli—The choices we make in different areas of our lives are stimuli and catalysts that act as incentives that directly or indirectly influence the events and transactions that transpire in our lives.

Our choices have the power to cause change in any area of our lives. The choices we make are stimuli that act as agents that initiate change in different areas of our lives.

Our choices are catalysts that trigger the actions and reactions that transpire in the streets of life.

The choices we make personally, and the choices other people make on our behalf have the ability to act as stimuli in our lives to orchestrate the changes and events in our lives. The choices we and others make on our behalf in one aspect of life or another are able to cause reactions and changes in different areas of our lives. Our choices act as stimuli that influence, control, and determine our experiences and results in all spheres of life.

Our Choices Are Inhibitors—The choices we make can become inhibitors in our lives and in the lives of others. Their effects are two-sided and, as such, they can result in beneficial or detrimental outcomes. Whatever the choices we make effectuate in our lives and in the lives of others depends on what the choice entails and the intent that propels us to make the choices in the first place.

The choices we make in different areas of our lives can become inhibitors for good or evil in our lives and the lives of others. They can have a positive or negative influence and impact; it all depends on the reason behind our choices.

Our choices can become inhibitors in our lives that prevent or stop us from accessing the necessary opportunities that would have helped us to progress in life. The choices we make can also act as inhibitors that halt, stop, and bring to an end the negative happenings in our lives and the lives of others. Our choices as inhibitors, can produce positive or negative outcomes in our lives and in the lives of others.

- *Choices as Positive Inhibitors*—The choices of a person, family, community, an organization, or a country have the power to become inhibitors to stop the pains, agony, shame, reproach, to wipe away the tears from people's faces, and to bring an end to the negative happenings in their lives. For example, when a person makes the choice to stand up to a bully. He or she has become an inhibitor to bullying. He or she has become a positive inhibitor who stops and frustrates bullies from fulfilling their bullying agendas. Choices as positive inhibitors can have tremendous impacts and change the course of events in the lives of people for good, especially when the intentions are selfless and for the benefit of humanity.

- *Choices as Negative Inhibitors*—The choices we make personally or collectively as a group can become negative inhibitors in our lives and in the lives of others. When people individually or collectively engage in making poor, illicit, or bad choices, they place limitations over themselves that will eventually halt their progress and growth in life. They become determinants that deflect their progress and success in life.

    Such choices have the power to hold people as hostages. When choices become negative inhibitors, they keep people from accessing opportunities and possibilities in life. These kinds of choices can cause standstills in the lives of an individual, family, community, or a nation.

In all realms of life, the choices we make either work as positive or negative inhibitors in our lives, and we must be mindful of the choices we are making because the choices we make have the power to work for us or against us.

Our choices are like magnetic fields that attracts and repels things in our lives.

Our Choices Are Like Magnets—The choices we make in different areas of our lives are our invisible magnets that draw things into our lives. Whatever transpires in our lives is anchored on the choices we make and those that others make on our behalf. Our choices eventually determine the inflow of resources in our lives. These can be human, financial, intellectual, mental, and/or spiritual resources, depending on the choices we make in different spectrums of life.

Our choices are like invisible magnets that draw things into our lives.

Just as magnets will always attract certain metals, our choices can attract good or bad things, into our lives or they can repel good or bad things from our lives. Our choices in any sphere of life have a magnetic power to control and determine what transpires and surges into our lives.

Our Choices Are Taskmasters—In the race of life and in the Maze of Choices, the choices we make in different areas of our lives dictate the course of our lives, because we live our lives by the choices we make, and others make on our behalf.

This is the reality that we as humans live out daily. Our choices carry elements of rewards or retributions, depending on what the choices we make entail. When the choices we make carry the elements of rewards or retributions and recompense, they become realities in our lives. When our choices carry elements of retribution, they become the taskmasters that enforce the actualization of the punishments and penalties that the choices entail.

Our choices have the power to become taskmasters in our lives to enforce the fulfillment of their consequences. They eventually dictate the course of our lives and the events that transpires in our lives. They often become our taskmasters without us even realizing it.

Sadly, most people have become slaves and victims of their choices, and their choices throw them curveballs, instead of paving the way for them to achieve progress in life.

All activities and transactions that transpire in our lives are orchestrated by the choices we make individually or collectively. Whether we are aware of it or not, our choices either work for us or work against us. The most disheartening aspects of our choice's being taskmasters is that some of us, if not all of us, in one area or another in our lives have become the victims of our choices or victims of the choices that others have made on our behalf. We all have to accept the fact that the choices of others can becomes our taskmasters and make life unbearable and burdensome for us; hence, we must be mindful of the choices we make.

> *Prayer is the weapon (machete) for clearing the way*
> *and making a way where there is no way.*
> *—Edo Proverb*

Our Choices Are Our Pathfinders—The choices we make in different affairs of our lives goes ahead of us as forerunners to prepare the way for our arrival. Whatever reception we might receive is being determined by the choices we've made in the past.

The good, right, and just choices we make in different areas of our lives act as pathfinders in paving the way for us to accelerate and progress in life. Just as prayer is a weapon (machete) for clearing and creating a path, our choices are weapons we use to create and prepare our paths in life.

Whatever position or location we might find ourselves in today and in the future is being orchestrated by the choices we've made in the past and the choices we are making now. Every time we make a choice, we create a path and embark on the route we have created, and the choices other people make, whether good or bad, can also have the ability to create pathways in our lives with or without our permission.

In all of our dealings in life, our choices align us with our futures by going ahead of us to discover, create, map, and enlist opportunities for us, and give us access to new possibilities. They can also delete us from the possibilities and opportunities in life.

CHOICES ARE FORERUNNERS

Our choices act as our street- lights, that illuminate our paths through life. How bright and illuminated our paths are in life is anchored on the choices we make and sometimes in the choices, others make on our behalf. The content of our choices determines the paths that are being created for us and the brightness of our paths.

If we are not satisfied with our present route that our choices have created for us, it is never too late to reroute our path in life by making choices that will help us create and find a new path that will be beneficial to us and others.

Our Choices Are Repellents—Our choices in life act as repellents in our lives and in the lives of others. They can repel either good or bad things from our lives, depending on what our choices entail. One wrong or bad choice can become a repellent that drives or deflects good and viable opportunities from our lives, and from families, communities, companies, and even countries.

In contrast, one good or right choice can also be a repellent that prevents negative happenings and events from occurring in our lives and in the lives of others and shield us from adversities, and curve balls in life.

On the flip side, our choices, as repellents, can also be weapons that cut short our opportunities and possibilities. Our choices have the power to determine what we can access and what can't access us.

The choices we make can become repellents that drive the forces of negative influences from our lives or become repellents that delete good things from our lives. A choice can be a positive repellent for our good and benefit or a negative repellent for our downfall and detriment.

In all the affairs of life, our choices have their own implications and benefits in our lives. Our choices either implicate or benefit us. We design and redesign our lives by our choices; we are the "choice-smiths" of our lives.

We are the goldsmiths and silversmiths of our lives. We fashion our lives by our choices. We are the "choice-smiths" of our lives.

Choice-smith—By the choices we make in different affairs of life, we all have become the choice-smiths of our lives. Just like goldsmiths and blacksmiths who create objects from metals, our choices create and make different things in our lives and in the lives of others. Our choices create, hammer, redesign, shape, and reshape our lives.

Our choices, whether good or bad, right or wrong, wise or foolish, are the fabric that we use to create our realities.

We fashion the affairs of our lives by the choices we make, individually or collectively. Whether we are aware of it or not, we are constantly creating, designing, and redesigning the events and transactions that transpire in our lives through our choices.

Our lives evolve and revolve around the choices we make, and our choices, whether good or bad, right or wrong, wise or foolish, are the fabric that we use to create our realities. We are the choice-smiths of our lives and whatever choices we make produce things in our lives that become the realities of our lives. Just as the goldsmith makes gold jewelry, our choices create different experiences, happenings, situations, and outcomes in our lives. Other people's choices can also create different experiences and outcomes in our lives. One way or the other, we and others are the choice-smiths in the affairs of our lives.

Human beings are empowered to create, design, repair, and remodel their lives via the power of choice, and as choice-smiths in our individual lives, we control, direct, and redirect the affairs and issues in our lives.

Finally, by the force of choice, we are the goldsmiths, silversmiths, and locksmiths in our lives by the choices we make. Just as the blacksmith and goldsmith create things of beauty, we have become choice-smiths who can create things of value, treasure, beauty, and honor in our lives. By the choices we make, we become the locksmiths in our lives and in the lives of others, who open or lock the doors of opportunities, possibilities, favor, and sometimes the doors of mishaps and disasters.

We are designing and redesigning our lives by the choices we make.

We should not make ourselves or others the victims of our choices.

Refuse to Be the Victim of Your Choices—Sometimes in life we might have to make some hard, tough, and painful choices: however, it is vital not to make ourselves or others the victims of our choices. We must be mindful of the choices we make because most of the time, we are not aware of the power and the influence our choices can have in making us and others their victims.

Just as we cannot run away from our shadows, likewise we cannot run away from our choices or separate our realities from our choices. Unfortunately, some of us have made ourselves and others the victims of our choices. It is crucial to be sensitive and positively intentional in making choices, especially the choices that have to do with life, in order not to make ourselves and others the victims of our choices. We must be mindful of our choices because we all will eat the fruits of the choices we make.

We live by our choices. We cannot run away from our shadows nor can we run away from our choices.

> "There are no empty choices. Our choices are embedded either with redemption, rewards, compensation, or retribution. This is why we must make wise choices."

CHAPTER 14

CHOOSE YE

WE LIVE OUR lives based on a compilation of the choices we've made and acted upon; hence, we all live our lives by the choices we make. Some of these choices are made only once, while others are made once and again.

Every day we make choices that will eventually make us who we are. Life always presents to every one of us the possibility to choose from the various options available at every situation, circumstance, issue of life, and whatever we choose becomes our choice. We are solely responsible for the choices we make in spite of the prevailing circumstances.

It is crucial to be aware of the fact that our choices are not dormant but active forces in our lives and in the lives of others. Once the choice wheel has been set in motion, via the choices we make, our choices have the power to become recurring decimals in our lives that will eventually control and dictate our lot in life.

Every day, when we make choices to love or to hate, to be joyful or depressed, to be generous or selfish, to be kind or wicked, to be law-abiding or unlawful, to forgive or not to forgive, to respect or to disrespect, to dignify or to abase, to honor or to dishonor, and so we create our world and the events that will transpire in the streets of life. Whatever we choose is our choice, and it will become our reality because there are no empty choices.

> **Every wave of the sea doesn't come empty but carries things to the shores, which can be treasures or trash. Likewise, the choices we make are not empty but are embedded with rewards or consequences, which are translated into events and happenings in our lives.**

There Are No Empty Choices—In the Maze of Choices, there are no empty choices, neither are there empty words. Every choice we make is embedded with something known as an outcome, and this outcome can have a positive or negative effect on our lives. The conscious and subconscious choices we make can carry temporary, long-lasting, or everlasting redemption, rewards, repercussions, or retributions, which will eventually shape the events and happenings that transpires in our lives.

In the race of life, our choices create our paths in life, and they create the occurrences in our live, and the atmospheric conditions around us. Consider how the choices we make with the words below determine the kind of transactions that transpire in our lives and in the streets of life.

- Accept and Reject
- Black and White
- Bless and Curse
- Find and Lost
- Free and Bind
- Give and Take
- Good and Evil
- Honor and Abuse

- Joy and Sad
- Kind and Rude
- Love and Hate
- Rich and Poor
- Success and Failure

Ironically, each of the options in each line above carries equal letters, and whatever word we choose to use in our dealings with ourselves and other people will determine the events or happenings that occurs in our lives and our society. Therefore, the choices we make are not empty, and we are custodians of our choices.

> **The choices we make in any given situation either empower or disarm us.**

We Are the Custodians of Our Choices—We are the custodians of the choices we make. Whatever we do with our power of choice is our responsibility. Whether other factors influence the choices we make or not, we are responsible for our choices. We, as human beings, have the power to make choices in the affairs of our lives, and we have the power individually and collectively as a group to pull the choice triggers in the issues that pertain to us.

Choices are investments and deposits for future occurrences and eventualities that will transpire in our lives and in the lives of others, and the choices we make as investors in the Maze of Choices will determine our dividends and outcomes in the race of life. Whatever we choose to invest via the choices we make will eventually determine our buoyancy in life, irrespective of external or internal influences.

> **The choices we make either enhance or impede our future.**

The Choices We Make Are Deposits

Every choice we make today is a deposit into our future. Choices are the raw materials for the transactions that will transpire tomorrow. Today's choice deposits are our down payments for tomorrow's transactions in our lives, which will be translated into experiences, events, or occurrences in our lives.

The choice deposits we've made in the past are the triggers for our current experiences in life, because the series of choices made are propellers of the events and transactions that transpire in our lives today.

We all, as humans, have made a series of choice deposits in the affairs of life in the past, which have eventually accumulated to create our current experiences and realities. The choices we make individually or collectively have the power to put us on course or off course in life.

In any area of life where we experience a change, whether a positive or negative change, there is always the possibility that our choices from the past have created the opening for the current change we are experiencing right now.

The choices we make individually or collectively have a way of interfering with our welfare and experiences in life, and the choices we make personally and collectively can directly or indirectly affect and influence the general well-being of each and every one of us. However, the choices we make personally have the power to act as succors in minimizing the shock waves and damages the choices of others might trigger in our lives. Hence, we are major stakeholders of our choices; that is why we all will live by the choices we make.

At the end of the day, we make choices; and our choices will eventually make us who we are. Ultimately, we live by our choices.

We Will Live by Our Choices—Choice-making is an empowerment, especially when the power of choice is deployed appropriately. Every day, our choices have the power to make us by influencing and shaping our outcomes in life. Just as we shall live by our faith, each and every one of us will live by the choices we make. Every chapter, phase, and stage in our lives is determined by the choices we make.

Whatever we become in life is determined by our choices and how colorful the chapters of our lives are, is anchored on the choices we make. Our choices are our forerunners, which can become our pathfinders or stumbling blocks and obstacles in our lives. Whatever crosses our path in life is proportional to the choices we have made. At the end of the day, we make choices, and our choices will eventually make us who we are. Ultimately, we will live by our choices.

Whatever we become in life is orchestrated by the choices we make. That is why the choices we make decide our successes or setbacks in life. Every choice we make has the inherent power to affect us positively or negatively. Certain privileges in life can be missed because of the choices we, and others make, and certain potholes can be averted by the choices we make.

The choices we make can create potholes in our paths in the race of life.

Potholes in the Race of Life—In life's journey, the choices we make construct our paths and pave the way for us in all endeavors of life. The choices we make personally, and others make on our behalf can create potholes in our paths in the race of life.

How we sail through life is dependent on the choices we make. Whether our journey will be smooth or rough in life is orchestrated by our choices, and certain potholes of life can be avoided by the choices we make, especially when we consciously and intentionally make choices that are good, just, and right, in spite of the compelling, external influences that might want to corrupt our power of choice.

In order to avert potholes in our lives, we must place certain spiritual, moral, and social values on our lives and then live by such values. These values should be vividly engraved in our hearts because these values will become our mirrors and golden rule that guards all choices.

Our choices are our navigators, which we use to navigate through situations and circumstances in the journey of life.

Our Choices Are Our Life Navigators

In life, choices are a mode of transportation and they are a navigating tool for our life's journey. Our choices determine our success or failure at different phases of our lives. Whether we are falling, crawling, leaping, jumping, running, flying, or soaring in life is determined by the choices we make.

Our choices have the power to plan, direct, and redirect the course of our lives. We can be put on course or off course by the choices we make because at each point in life, the choices we make act as the navigators, maps, or compasses that will route us to our destinations over time.

In spite of external interferences, our choices amid situations and challenges of life have the power to direct and reroute our outcomes in all spheres of our lives. No matter our position and status in life, our choices are what navigates us to where we in life. If peradventure we are not satisfied by our location or position in life, we can make choices that will reroute our lives to where we want to be.

In the streets of life, choices are the navigating tools that initiate changes in any sphere of life. Choice is a vital force that is applicable in all transactions in all areas of life. Our choices are our messengers and forerunners that go ahead of us into our tomorrow. God has given to every one of us the power to map out and navigate our lives as we desire through our choices.

Our choices can become turning points that move us from one phase of life to another.

Choices as Transitions and Turning Points—In life, we all have made some bad, poor, or wrong choices. However, the gravity of the poor, wrong, or bad choices might differ from person to person and situation to situation. Yet, the truth remains: we all have been guilty of not making the perfect choice at one point and another in our lives.

Our imperfect choices eventually create situations and happenings in our lives that might slow us down, stagnate us, or place us in situations that are not conducive for us. These choices might cause some discomfort, dissatisfaction, discontentment, and sometimes pain and regret.

Regardless of the situations or happenings that our choices create in our lives, we still have a choice to make amid the prevailing situations. The choice we make amid our present situations can become a turning point in our lives, either for our good or downfall. We can only get out of any bad or unpleasant situations created by our past choices by making better choices that will reroute us.

Our choices amid situations of life are our transition passages and the turning points in the race of life.

It is crucial to make choices that will ensure our survival and transition from the bad places the poor or bad choices we made in the past have placed us. Our choices directly or indirectly navigate us around the bends and curveballs of life and in the process, they create the landscapes of our lives.

The choices we make have the power to initiate us into the realm of success or failure.

Our Choices Are Initiators—Every action and transaction that takes place in any sphere of life is initiated by the choices people make daily as they walk the street of life. Personal or collective choices always set a wheel in motion that initiates a process which creates profitable and unprofitable outcomes.

Every choice has the inherent power to initiate profits and losses in people's lives. Every action and reaction in the streets of life is propelled by our choices. Our choices initiate all the transactions that take place in our lives, and they can start a chain reaction that might eventually result in domino effects. In each case, the effects can be productive or unproductive.

In as much as the choices we make are initiators of our outcomes in life, our intentions are catalysts in paving the way for the choices we make in all realms of life. Intention is a major facilitator that propels and initiates every choice, and the intent behind a choice acts as an initiator that facilitates the choice-making.

It is crucial to ponder and weigh the intent of our hearts before making any choice. This will help us in making choices that will initiate more positive, productive, and profitable outcomes. When our intentions are put on a scale of pondering, it initiates the possibility to choose rightly.

Our Intention as the Initiator of Choices—*Intention* simply means the "why" behind the choices we make. Intentions can differ from person to person and from situation to situation. Whatever is our intention for making the choices we make will determine the outcome of the choice. In all issues of life, our intentions can be

- Caring or Harmful
- Good or Evil
- Selfish or Selfless
- Welfare or Warfare

Our intentions in the Maze of Choices are forerunners that influences the choices we make per time and situations. When our intentions are good, we will certainly make good choices and when our intentions are evil, we will make bad choices that will always reflect evil deeds.

To React, Respond, or Ignore? —There comes a time when we all make choices to either ignore, react, or respond to different situations in our lives. At one stage or another, we all might have gone through the phase of ignoring, reacting, or responding to issues. There are situations and happenings that will occur in our lives that confront our power to choose. Whatever we choose to do becomes our choice by the actions we take.

In most situations our choices amid the challenges of life reflect whether we are reacting, responding, or ignoring something. This is especially true in unpleasant situations such as when someone offends or upset us. Whatever we choose to do at that point in time is being anchored by our power of choice.

It might surprise us to know that reacting, responding, or ignoring any wrongdoing is by choice. In all transactions that transpire in the streets of life, our choices are the underlying dominant factors that propel all of our dealings in life.

Our reactions or responses to people and situations are liable to our power of choice, and they are choices we all are making, consciously or subconsciously as we walk the streets of life.

> ***Our choices amid the situations and happenings of life unleash the transactions that transpire in our lives.***

Our Choices Are Transactions—The choices we make are transactions, which are processed into events, issues, experiences, and happenings that eventually produce rewards or consequences in our lives. The processing period might differ from one choice to another; however, choices get processed, whether we are aware of it or not. The choices we make in different areas of life are compiled and translated into happenings in our lives.

Any time we engage our power of choice in any issue, we are either directly or indirectly carrying out a transaction process. Once the process has taken its full course, it is translated into different happenings and events in our lives. The processing time might differ, like any other transactions, but outcomes always ensue.

The most profound thing about choices is that our choices are transactions in our lives and in the lives of others.

Our choices amid situations and happenings of life unleash the transactions that transpire in our lives. Even in trivial things of life, the choices we make are translated into experiences and outcomes that have the power to resound and reverberate in other areas of our lives.

Most of the time, we are not willing to face the results of the bad or poor choices we've made in the past. Whether we are willing or not, we and others who are in the radius of the choices we've made will eventually pay the price for our choices, because choices are not defunct but extant in nature.

Choices are not defunct but extant in nature.

The choices we make always have a way of catching up with us, and sometimes we are not prepared for our reunion with our past choices. Unfortunately, the reality is we cannot escape or refuse the reunion of our past choices with us.

The Choice Reunion

Most times in life, we individually or collectively have the option to choose if we will want to attend the reunions, we receive invitations to from different walks of life. Such invitations can be a reunion of old schoolmates, sport teams, old colleagues, churches, families, and more.

In such cases, we collectively or individually have the option to accept or ignore the reunion invitation. But in life, the reality is the choices we've made in the past have a way of reuniting with us without our permission. This is true because the choices we make in different spheres of life are not defunct but extant in nature.

The choices we've made in the past have a way of catching up with us and most times, they come unannounced and unexpected. This is the reality most of us are not conscious about and not prepared for, especially the reunion of the poor or bad choices we made.

As we journey through life, there comes a time in each of our lives when the choices we've made in the past are eagerly waiting for our arrival. Whatever is the reception we eventually receive is being orchestrated by the choices we've made in the past and what the choices we made entail.

Just as some of us are not so excited about going to reunion parties because of past experiences or happenings, likewise, most of us are not willing or happy to re-unite with the choices we made in the past, especially the bad, and ill choices.

Just as we cannot separate ourselves from our shadows, we cannot reject or resist the reunion party or the punishment of the choices we've made in the past. In life, there is always a reunion taking place between us and the choices we've made in the past. Even though we are not always prepared or ready to meet with the consequences of the poor, ill, or bad choices made in the past, the reunion is guaranteed once the choices have been made. However, if the choices we made in the past were good, just, and right, there is always a jubilation that accomplishes our reunion with our past choices.

It is crucial for us to be conscious of this fact, that as we engage in making choices in one area of life and another, we are unknowingly issuing invitation letters to ourselves for a reunion party or reunion of punishment that will take place in our future. This is the reality that we must be conscious of, so that when the reunion with the choices made in the past surfaces or takes place, it will not meet us unprepared.

The reverberation of the choices we made yesterday is like a coin that is two-sided. Such choices can have a beneficial or adverse effect on all aspects of our lives. Therefore, our experiences and outcome at the reunion of our past choices with us depends on what the choices we made entail, which can be a reunion of celebration or of punishment.

Every choice we make has the potency to reverberate and, most of the time, the outcome is unknown and unpredictable.

Our choices are a major trigger for the metamorphoses that transpire in our lives and in the world.

Choices Are Agents of Change

We live in a world where things are continuously undergoing metamorphoses, and one of the major triggers for this is our choices, because choices are triggers for change in all spheres of life.

Change occurs in life as a result of the choices we make at every junction in life. The choices we make amid the challenges of life have the power to initiate a change and the changes that will occur will be determined by the content of the choice made.

The sequence of choices we make are the catalysts for the change in our lives. Actions are the activators and converters that translate a choice into a substance that is tangible. This eventually produces our experiences in life. Every choice we make regarding an issue or situation acts as a converter of the atmospheric condition that is present in our lives.

In any area of life, we desire a change; our choices are the agents that will create the desired change in our lives. The outcome or result of the choices that we make is seen in our lives and our streets. Making flippant choices make us sail on dangerous waters because our choices are the converter that turns situations around either for good or bad.

In all aspects of our lives as human beings, our choices act as our catalysts and stimuli that initiate change. Sometimes it will initiate a desired change or an undesired change. The choices we make have the inherent power to initiate a change in our lives because change is at the mercy of the choices we've made, which are being regulated by time.

In as much as change is crucial for our survival and growth as human beings, it is important to know that change is time oriented. That is why every change that needs to take place must be done at the appropriate time, because when the timeframe for a particular change has elapsed, it might be difficult or impossible to make a change. Just as we cannot change yesterday or retrieve yesterday, also there are certain things in life that our choices cannot change when the window of time is closed.

That is why choices might be the agent of change, but choices are time oriented. Choice might be an agent of change, but choices are guided and dependent on time.

Therefore, choices made within a stipulated timeframe determine positive changes in any area of life. According to the common say, strike the iron while the iron is still hot. Likewise, in life, there are certain choices that must be made within a timeframe because once the window or curtain of time has closed, such choices might be impossible to make or it might be too late to make them.

Certain choices are time oriented and time sensitive. Ignoring the importance of time is like courting disaster, and this, can result in tears and irrevocable regrets.

Choices Are Time Oriented

There are certain choices in life that are time-oriented and time-sensitive. These choices must be made within the stipulated timeframe. Any attempt to ignore the stipulated time for the choices to be made can result in minor or grievous outcomes. Sometimes, these outcomes cannot be reversed, especially when the window of time has closed.

While we live in the era of grace, there comes a time in our lives where the era of grace will be over and the choices, we refused to make becomes irrevocable, because all the choices we make in life are time oriented. This is why we must honor, love, and respect our parents while they are still alive and why it is important to love, cherish, spend, and invest time in our children or spouse. It is also why we must appreciate and respect opportunities, people, and profitable relationships in our lives. Above all, it is why we must say the prayer of salvation while there is still time.

It is crucial for us to know that some choices in life cannot be pushed aside or postponed, because the flight of life is on a continuous cruise mode. Our time is always soaring once it takes off until our time on earth is over.

Choices Are the Accelerator and Brake of Life—The choices we make in different areas of our lives act as our accelerators and brakes, which we use to navigate and maneuver through the issues of life. It is crucial to know that the choices we make can accelerate us in the right direction or derail us in life's journey, and the choices we've made can also be the brake that halts our progress in life or delivers us from dangers.

In all spheres of life, our choices can be summoned up as accelerators or brakes in our lives. The choices we make in different areas of our lives act as brakes in our lives to interrupt and stop the sequence and course of issues or events in our lives. Our choices can also become a force in our lives that halts our progress, like a brake that stops the influx of relevant traffic or opportunities. This will eventually lead to stagnation in our lives. Our choices can also act as brakes that stop us and help us avert dangers in our lives.

On the other hand, the choices we make can act as accelerators in our lives, which move us to success in the areas of life where we have made choices that are empowering and profitable to us. Our choices determine our speed in different endeavors of life.

The choices we make, and sometimes the choices others make on our behalf, affect our pace in the affairs of life. We can be crawling, leaping, walking, running, flying, or soaring in our respective endeavors, but we need to have an inner circle who we can discuss things with, in the Maze of Choices in order to see things from different perspectives. This will help us to avoid making choices that will either make us or others the victims of our choices.

We make choices and the choices we've made will eventually embrace us.

Inner Circle (Checks and Balances)—Choice-making is a vital and integral part of us as human beings. Choice-making is a huge part of our existence because we all are daily engaging in making choices in different affairs of our lives to route and reroute our lives. Whatever choices we make will directly influence the standards of our lives, because we all are living our lives by the choices we make. Life is lived based on the compilation of the choices we made.

Making bad, poor, or wrong choices and not realizing it is the most dangerous thing we can do individually or collectively in life. We need people in our lives who will be there to scold, correct, or guide us as we journey through the Maze of Choices in the affairs of our lives. As we journey through the paths of life, the choices we make will become our realities and they will eventually determine how we sail through life.

CHOICES ARE FORERUNNERS

It is vital for us to have people in our lives who will be there to guide and help us to make choices that will not be detrimental to our future and the futures of those close to us.

> **What an elder will see while sitting down, a child will not see it even when the child climbs the top of a tree.**
> **—Edo Proverb**

As human beings, we depend on each other for our survival. Having people in our lives is essential and crucial, because none of us can live our lives without the input or wisdom of another person.

That is why we need people in our lives who will act as checkers in our lives and who will always tell us the truth, even if the truth is a bitter pill that we might not want to swallow. Having, people in our lives helps us see things from different perspectives and helps us to minimize the possibility of making irrational choices.

Also, people can mentor, guide, educate, and encourage us at the very points in life where we need guidance. We need people who will stand up to correct us when we are going off course. We need others to bring us to order when necessary and we need people in our life that will reroute and re-direct us in the Maze of Choices to bring checks and balances to our choices.

Lastly, we need some people in our inner circle who can help us to engage the force of foresight in the Maze of Choices. Especially in the areas of life where we lack knowledge. Engaging the force of foresight in making choices will helps us to predict the possible outcomes of the choices we make.

The Force of Foresight—In the Maze of Choices, having foresight is crucial in avoiding certain potholes in life. Seeing far and envisioning the rewards or consequences of any choice is vital to us, and it keeps us and others from being the victims of our choices.

Our ability to see far and beyond our current circumstances or challenges in the Maze of Choices is a game changer that helps us to avoid certain shame and pains during the choice reunions in life. Having foresight in any realm of life, while engaging our power of choice, will help us to envision the possibilities and dangers that are embedded in the choices we want to make.

Engaging the force of foresight in the Maze of Choices will enable us to choose rightly because choices carry a redemptive power with them. In the race of life, choices are our redemptive key that leads to second chances and that can allow us to make amends when necessary.

Most regrets and tears shed in life have to do with the choices we've made in the past.

Choices Are a Redemptive Force—In the race of life, we create the good and the bad events or happenings that transpire in our lives by the choices we make individually and collectively. Likewise, we correct our past mistakes and errors by the choices we make amid the present events or happenings in our lives. Such choices are a redemptive force that we use to correct past errors,

Most regrets and tears shed in life have to do with the choices we've made in the past. However, we can avert certain pains created by the choices made in the past by being truthful to ourselves that our former choices were wrong. We must admit when our choices from the past are responsible for the present chaos in our lives.

Our ability to face the truth and swallow the bitter pill of truth by engaging the redemptive key of choice to choose correctly, will have a tremendous, positive impact in our lives personally and collectively.

We all are redeemable by the choices we make. Choices gives us second chance to set right the wrong or bad choices from our past, especially when the window of time is still open in our favor.

CHOICES ARE FORERUNNERS

Every day, we are given the opportunity to make choices that will redeem us and others from the retributions of former poor and ill choices. By the power of redemption, which we commonly call a "second chance," we all are given the opportunity to use our power of choices as our reset and restart buttons in our life's journey.

Our choices can be our reset button in life and can allow us to start fresh.

Choices as Our Reset and Restart Button in Life—The choices we make in all spheres of life can be used as a reset -buttons, that create a new chapter in our lives, when we come to a place or point of standstill, disappointment, dissatisfaction, and frustration in life. The choices we all make at the junction of discontentment can reset and reroute our path to change the existing status quo.

In all endeavors of life, the choices we make in different issues in our lives can act as reset buttons to set things right or make things go wrong. Whatever might be the issue of concern in our lives individually or collectively as a group, the choices we make regarding various issues of concern will determine the outcome.

The choices we make have the power to reboot and empower us to make a fresh start when the window of time is still open. In every aspect of our lives, whether spiritual, physical, financial, or social, our choices set the course of events in our lives and sometimes in the lives of others.

Wherever we might be today in our individual lives or collectively as a group, has been determined by our choices. When we make choices that initiate a change, they act as our reset buttons in the affairs of life. Choices give us the opportunity to start fresh and to change and turn around the undesirable aspects of our lives for the better.

Choices as restart buttons give us the possibilities in areas of our lives where the window of time has not been closed to make amends for a new beginning that will engender the desired results or outcomes in the areas where choices have been made to reset our course in life.

Continuously engaging the power of choice positively to reboot our lives is important. By choice, we can make a tremendous difference in our lives by turning unpleasant issues or situations in our lives to our own advantage. The truth is, at one point or another in each of our lives, individually or corporately, we all will need to use the reset button of choice to put things right and in perspective in our lives.

The choices we make individually or corporately amid chaos, desperation, contention, stability, abundance, or success, can reset the course of events in our lives and make a difference by bringing us to new chapters in our lives whereby we can grow and soar.

In all affairs of life, we should pray for the grace to make right choices each and every day. This is important because the choices we make, individually or collectively as a group, are our forerunners in life.

It is in our own interest to choose rightly in order to avert the possibility of setting a wrong wheel in motion in our lives. By using the reset button of choices, we can make a fresh start, especially in areas of our lives where we might have missed out due to poor or bad choices. We must choose rightly while the window of time is still open, and in our favor, because there is time for everything, and our choices are at the mercy of time.

Once the window of time is closed, the gift and freedom to choose or make choices in any sphere of life will be over. We should endeavor to choose rightly while time is in our favor, because choosing rightly makes us a resource and a channel of blessings to ourselves and to others.

Finally, we all will live by the choices we make. Just as a man cannot run away from his shadow, likewise we cannot run away from the choices we've made.

IN LIFE, WE have many choices to choose from for different situations. Some choices can result in either good or bad outcomes. Sometimes, we cannot predict the outcome of the choices we make, but we can envision the outcome of those choices to some extent. Just as we cannot see the end of a maze, likewise we cannot see the end course of our choices.

That is why choices are like mazes, where we have multiple options and paths to choose from, but the path we take will determine whether we are advancing or being halted in our journey. It is wise to make good choices, even in tough situations. The outcome of the good, just, and right choices we make outweighs the temporary discomfort some choices might cause. The choices are up to us to make.

J. Ekhator

DAILY CHOICE NUGGETS

1. "The choices we make today in different areas of our lives have the power to alter the course of our lives."

2. "Our lives are built on the choices we make, and we will live by our choices."

3. "Our choices are the forerunners of rewards or consequences that we are answerable to. No one can escape the rewards or consequences of the choices he or she has made."

4. "Life on earth is a race and the race of life is being run by the choices we make."

5. "In the race of life, we progress and increase our value by the choices we make. Likewise, retrogression is trigged and established by the choices make."

6. "The value we place on ourselves and others are seen in the choices we make consistently."

7. "Every experience, reward, consequence, and outcome in life are the collections and summaries of the choices we made in the past."

8. "At one point and the other in our life journeys, every one of us will certainly have to dance to the tune of themusic our choices have written and produced for us. It is a dance we cannot deny or ignore nor escape."

9. "In the Maze of Choices, there is no neutral ground, nor spectators; we are all participants, who are actively engaging our power of choice consciously and subconsciously."

10. "Of a truth, we will live by the choices we make individually and collectively. Unfortunately, the choices of others also directly and indirectly influence our lives; thus, to some degree, at one point or another, in life, we will also live by the choices of others."

11. "The choices we make in different areas of life can become our ceiling points, which eventually determine whether we are soaring or revolving around in the area where the choices were made."

12. "It is vital and mandatory to know and be conscious of the fact that every choice made has the possibility or prospect of causing a chain reaction in our lives and in the lives of others."

13. "In most affairs of life, we have the absolute power to choose but we do not have the absolute power to control or determine the outcome of the choices we've made."

14. "The intersection of the choices we made yesterday with our today creates the events and happenings that transpire in our lives."

15. "The collateral damage of bad, poor, and ill choices outweighs the temporal gratification."

16. "In every instruction, there is information, and, by choice, we unveil the information for our profit."

17. "Freedom to choose is a valuable treasure that is embedded with responsibility."
18. "Generational blessings, generational problems, and collateral damages are some of the successors of our choices."
19. "The reality in life is sometimes we have to pay the price for the bad choices made by others."
20. "Just because a choice is wrong, does not necessarily mean it's bad. Sometimes it just simply isn't the best option available for a given situation."
21. "Sometimes, we unconsciously make ourselves and others voluntary victims of circumstances because of the poor and bad choices we make."
22. "We are always held accountable by our choices, whether we are aware of it or not."
23. "Our experiences, outcomes, and results are pointers that validate whether the choices we made in any area of life were good, right, just, smart, bad, poor, or wrong choices."
24. "Every day we influence others by the choices we make. Likewise, we are also influenced by the choices made by other people."
25. "We can talk about our pasts and moments, but we can only speak to our futures by/via the choices we make today."
26. "Every activity that transpires in the streets of life hinges on the choices we make individually and collectively as a group."
27. "The choices we make are our emissaries deployed into our future."
28. "Our lives as human beings are time oriented; there are advantages and disadvantages that are embedded

CHOICES ARE FORERUNNERS

in time, which are unveiled in their seasons. Therefore, making the right choices at the appointed time birth the advantages of the season in our favor."

29. "By the choices we make, time is either in our favor or we are running out of time; hence, we all must be time-conscious in the Maze of Choices and work circumspectly."

30. "We can only invest in the moment and the future because we cannot invest in our pasts or yesterday, nor turn back time, neither can we retrieve yesterday. Hence, choose wisely."

31. "Every new day is an opportunity to correct the bad, poor, and ill choices of yesterday. We must endeavor to make the right and good choices today because today, we have been given the second chance to start all over again."

*Thank you, Lord, for You are my source of inspirations,
I am forever grateful.
Evelyn Ekhator*

Lightning Source UK Ltd.
Milton Keynes UK
UKHW040838210521
384111UK00001B/5